.

God's Battered Child

An abused daughter's journey to God

By

April Lorier

Copyright © 2007 by April Lorier

ISBN 0-7414-3896-8

Published by:

INFI∞ITY
PUBLISHING.COM

1094 New DeHaven Street, Suite 100
West Conshohocken, PA 19428-2713
Info@buybooksontheweb.com
www.buybooksontheweb.com
Toll-free (877) BUY BOOK
Local Phone (610) 941-9999
Fax (610) 941-9959

Printed in the United States of America

Printed on Recycled Paper

Published March 2007

Chapters

From the Author

Any similarities to anyone living or dead are coincidental. **This is my story.** I lived it and I wrote about it to help other survivors of childhood abuse.

Much of the material was taken from my personal journals which I entitled **<u>Bruised, Battered, and Blessed</u> ©1993.** Also included in this book is material from poems written during my teens and early adulthood.

In 1973 I founded C.O.P.E., Inc., a non-profit organization for the retraining of abusive parents. Founded on the twelve principles of AA, we used professional therapists to oversee the training of our peer counselors. Offending parents were then sent to COPE instead of having their children removed.

My testimony before the California State Legislature contributed to passage of the 1974 Mandatory Reporting of Child Abuse and Neglect Law.

DEDICATED...

foremost to my three bundles of love, Mark, John, and Clarissa;

to all the surrogates God placed in my life: Margaret who encouraged me during my school years, and Liliane, my God-mother who shepherded me;

to my God-sisters Patty, Ann, Cheryl and Pat who accepted and encouraged me;

to my precious Grandmother "Frankie" who prayed God would send His angels to protect me;

to my favorite author Randall Arthur for his encouragement;

and to Nanette Snipes who shared her editor's eye over and over.

1 - WHEN A MAN LOVES A WOMAN

The steamer trunk was at least 120 years old and filled with contents that had been ordered burned sixty years ago. How did I end up with it? She taught me what a bad girl I was. She blamed me for her violent rages. And yet I had this gift, though the tag read, "For Marilyn." She never could accept my name change.

I wiped the black dust off my hands and picked up my glass of tea. The cold tea felt good on my dusty throat and I drank heartily. I swirled the tea and watched it dance in circles. "A lot like my life: circles," I thought. My reflection stared back from the side of the glass and I noticed how dirty my face was from digging through these grimy contents. As I continued staring at my reflection it seemed to swirl into her face in another place and time. . .

Her name was Claire Elise Foale, but those who knew her called her Elise. She often came to the skating rink that autumn of 1941, knowing most of the farm boys in Paw Paw and nearby Shabbona Grove would gather to meet girls. Rather than being content to huddle on the fringe like the other girls, she preferred to be the center of attention by weaving in and out of the other skaters, her long blonde hair flowing behind like a bride's veil. With blue eyes flashing like spring lightening, she would challenge the braver boys to race, then fill the room with her contagious laughter as each boy inevitably fell to defeat. She was wild and exciting, and all the boys fell under her spell and wanted her...

...especially Calvin Morston.

Elise was immediately taken by the bold young man who dared to challenge her. She remained smitten even after he had handily beaten her. His dark hair and mustache formed a perfect frame for mysterious hazel eyes, which would abruptly change to green without warning. She was also thrilled he was several inches taller than she. At 5'9" it was difficult to find a boy she could actually look up to.

They skated together most of the night until the rink's owner finally insisted they leave so he could close. They lingered in the parking lot sharing details of their lives, neither wanting to be the first to say goodnight.

Elise shared how she lived alone with her 72 year-old father, and how badly she missed her mother who had died of cancer two years earlier. She was seventeen and had one older sister, Olivia, who was married and living in Chicago. She loved playing baseball, riding her bicycle, roller skating, playing the piano, and drawing pictures of Betty Boop. In fact, she planned to become a dress designer and make a profession out of her drawing talent and sense of fashion. Not having any interest in cooking, sewing, or any of the "domestic stuff" women did, she much rather enjoyed the company of boys than other girls her age.

As it turned out, Calvin was also the youngest of his six brothers and sisters. He was nineteen and already holding down two jobs: a farmhand and a gas station attendant. He'd learned to cook from watching his mother and enjoyed creating new delicacies – especially desserts. Although his brothers regarded him as a "Goody-two-shoes," he admitted to Elise he wasn't really that good but just didn't get caught because he was so sneaky.

That night, he invited her out on their first date, a Halloween dance being held the following week. On Thanksgiving Day, he told her of his love for her. And in early December, two events transpired which would change both their lives forever: he invited her to his parents' home on Christmas, and the Japanese bombed Pearl Harbor.

That Christmas, Calvin proudly presented Elise to his family. He didn't mention Elise wasn't domestic. That would

2

only have worried his mother who had devoted her entire life to the care of her own family. He did, however, make sure to tell how Elise faithfully read her Bible every day, a fact that was sure to put his mother's mind at rest concerning Elise's upbringing. As always, Elise made quite an impression. She wore no make-up except pink lipstick, and her rosy cheeks gave her the glow of a true natural beauty. She played to every member of Calvin's family with dancing eyes, obviously enjoying every preening moment. Calvin marveled at her ability to manipulate the emotions of his stoic father and quiet country-bred mother; but he also noticed how she spent more time socializing with his brothers than his sisters. He worried they would be offended by this behavior and refuse to accept her. Still, he was hopelessly captivated by Elise and did not intend to let her get away. He proposed marriage to her that very night. She accepted.

In June of 1942, Elise became Mrs. Calvin Levi Morston. Times were hard, so only four people attended the small ceremony held in the parsonage of her pastor. As Calvin promised to love, honor, and protect her forever, Elise studied the face of her soon-to-be husband. He looked so handsome standing there. She had learned to appreciate his kind spirit and natural willingness to listen. He was always so sensitive about not hurting others' feelings, but was also ready to fight for her whenever needed. Because of her sister's unfaithful husband, she knew how lucky she was to find someone who wanted only her. He was just as competitive as she – a necessary trait if he was to gain her respect. His comical antics kept her laughing most of the time. She needed to laugh, just as she needed to be "number one" in somebody's life. Calvin was her answer and she fueled his passion without mercy.

Of course, he could use some fine-tuning to shape those rough edges. He drank a little, a habit that made her nervous because of her memories of searching in bars for her father. But Elise was sure with a little time she could convince him not only to give up his beer, but also those filthy cigarettes. After all, he was crazy about her, wasn't he?

A smile crept across Elise's face. Yes, Calvin Morston, with his Clark Gable looks and Tennessee Ernie Ford heart, was a real catch in any girl's opinion. With a little help from her, he would be perfect.

With little money to spend, Calvin and Elise spent the first month of their married life with his parents. Calvin set out to find a better-paying job so they could have their own apartment. Life was cozy and simple: church on Sundays with Calvin's mother, weekdays at the Wurlitzer Plant, and evenings and weekends alone together in bed.

But after only ten months of marriage, Elise found herself waving good-bye to her husband as he marched off to serve his country. She left for Chicago to live with her sister until she could join him again. Soon, she hoped.

It was not a happy time for Elise. She hated living with her bossy sister, but not as much as she hated the way her brother-in-law kept coming on to her.

Most of all, she was bothered by Olivia's attitude toward Calvin. She listened grimly as her sister talked about Calvin as if he were a hayseed. She poked fun at how he would say everything was "swell" in his letters. Elise didn't want her sister to know Calvin had only a sixth grade education, so she deliberately corrected his grammar when she read parts of his letters to Olivia.

Fights between the two sisters made Elise miss Calvin even more. Olivia kept reminding her how she could have gone to The Art Institute of Chicago and made something of her life. Their mother would have wanted Elise to receive the same education she had, she said. Instead Elise had married someone "without breeding" – so unlike their own father who had a business degree from Harvard, or their mother who was a schoolteacher. When Elise would bring up their father's drinking problem, her sister would tell her she deserved every time he had hit her. And when Olivia bragged about her own "catch" of a husband, Elise bit her tongue to keep from telling her what she knew about him. Then one day she blurted out the truth. Of course, her brother-in-law denied his inappropriate sexual behavior and demanded she leave "his" home at once. She did, and found refuge in the Baptist Home for Women where she lived until Calvin sent for her.

Eight months after Elise had waved good-bye to her husband, she boarded a train bound for El Paso, Texas, where Calvin was stationed at Biggs Field as a Surgical Technician. From her window seat she watched the passing scenery change from the brilliance of autumn red leaves to cactus growing on red clay.

Shortly after her arrival, they found a small second-floor apartment from which they could view only billboards. But they didn't care – they had eyes only for each other. Elise worked briefly at the PBX. Then she secured a position as secretary to their pastor, Rev J.C. Morehouse. It was then Elise first fell in love with the idea of Calvin becoming a pastor, especially when Rev. Morehouse mentioned what good "people skills" her husband had. She interpreted this to mean Calvin was a natural-born pastor. She began to share her dream with Calvin, who did not share her "vision." He hadn't yet learned how persuasive his wife could be when she put her mind to something.

In April of 1944, on her twenty-first birthday, Elise Morston delivered a blonde baby girl. Elise did not hear her baby's cries over her own screams for chocolate donuts and her dead mother. Her new baby was virtually ignored, as, once again, Elise demanded to be the center of attention.

I was that baby girl.

2 - THE CALLING

Because I was supposed to be a boy, my parents had not thought of any girls' names. One week after I was born, my mother saw the name of "Marilyn Mason" in the newspaper. My name became Marilyn, and five weeks later she returned to her secretarial position carting a baby buggy with me inside.

Six months later my father was released from active duty with a $450 bonus in his hands. His dream was to become self-employed with his own potato chip route. But a cold winter had cracked the block of his car and the money had to be spent to repair it. He was depressed as he saw his dream disappear, but my mother wasn't. She knew God was calling him to preach and viewed the cracked block as God's way of closing the door on any other profession. So Daddy took a job as a taxi driver, thinking he could save enough money to buy his route truck eventually.

But it wasn't to be. Mama was pregnant again, and in June of 1946, a second daughter was born. Her name was Janine Elaine.

I remember that day. My parents said they were going to get me a sister or brother, and then dropped me off at the home of strangers. I stood staring out the window for hours, my eyes barely clearing the sill. When they hadn't returned by bedtime, I knew they had given me away to these strangers because they liked their new baby better than me. Somehow, I knew it was because I was such a bad girl.

After Janine was born, Daddy was offered a job in El Paso as a Surgical Assistant at a well-known clinic. Because of his experience during the war, he was qualified to perform tonsillectomies, appendectomies, and work with burn victims. But even though the money offered was more than he ever dreamed of earning, Mama managed to talk him out of accepting the position. She saw this offer as a "trick of Satan" cleverly designed to deter Daddy from God's calling.

So Daddy drove a taxi for three more years, and then moved us to one of the largest cities in New Mexico where he accepted a position weighing trucks for the State. A druggist he met during this job told him the mission he attended was looking for a part-time pastor who had another means of support. Daddy was invited to preach a trial sermon and shortly after became their part-time pastor. Because he had served his country honorably, no one ever asked about his education. But I knew Daddy always felt insecure about his lack of education. It was a subject discussed between my parents only in whispers.

Mama skillfully used her musical talent to distance herself from the other church ladies, preferring to spend time with their musically-inclined children. As a result, she recruited several paying piano students.

I would have my fifth birthday while Daddy was at this mission. We shared a duplex with neighbors who had a swing set in their yard. They made it clear to Janine and me we were not allowed to swing on it. They knew Mama sent us outside every day so she could take a nap, and they resented her negligence as a mother. However, this assessment wasn't entirely fair. Since Janine's birth, Mama had begun experiencing numerous health problems, including blinding migraine headaches – a condition not helped by her diet of constant chocolate.

A week before my fifth birthday Mama was sick again. She told us to go next door and swing on the swing set since the neighbors were gone on vacation. But on the day before my birthday, they returned and the lady asked me point blank if we had played on her swing set while they were gone. I answered truthfully, as I had been taught to do.

By the time she and my mother finished screaming at each other, I knew I was in trouble. That night Mama told me I was a "bad girl" for betraying her and was canceling my birthday party. I cried, begged, and even enlisted the support of my father, which only resulted in a huge fight between them. Although Daddy made sure I had my party the next day, I believe it was *this* confrontation which made him decide never to challenge Mama's treatment of me again.

Under Daddy's leadership, the mission had grown from 24 to 110 members in one year. They could finally afford to pay a pastor full time. The very same druggist who had sent Daddy there in the first place was now advising the church board to pick someone else for pastor – "someone with experience." I remember hating church people for hurting my Daddy. It was the first time I'd ever seen him cry.

One month later, my father – still not ordained – accepted another part-time pastorate at a small church about three miles from the mission. During this time my parents were keeping Janine and I awake with violent arguments. Daddy, unwilling or unable to tolerate Mama's rages, would usually end up storming out of the house.

Mama had frequent rage tantrums like the ones she had seen her own alcoholic father have, and I seemed to annoy her more than Janine did. She spent most of the day in bed, getting up just in time to teach her piano students in the afternoon. She woke herself by eating chocolate and drinking coffee, a diet which caused her to be wide awake at midnight when Daddy came home exhausted.

I laid awake on these nights, praying God would find another home for me to live in. Janine just pulled her blankie closer and sucked her fingers more frantically.

It was one of those hot New Mexico afternoons when dry winds tossed tumbleweeds all over our yard and the afternoon sun tortured the cracked clay. I couldn't play on the swing next door, Mama and Janine were both asleep, and I was on the sidewalk, lonely and hot. Then I heard the far off tinkle of music from the ice cream truck! More than anything, I wanted a milk nickel. Surely Mama would have a nickel in her purse!

My blonde curls hung heavy with perspiration as I skipped up the gritty sidewalk leading to our front door. I knew it was time for Mama to get up and take her piano students, so I decided to risk bouncing into her darkened bedroom.

"Mama?" I whispered. "The big hand's on the nine and the little hand's on the two. It's time to get up and the ice cream truck is coming!"

"How many times have I told you not to bother me when I'm lying down?" Mama snapped back. "And why are you so dirty? You want all the neighbors to think we're not fit for the church?" Mama's face was red and her eyes became a pair of light blue slits. "Why aren't you in bed, anyway?"

"It's too hot, Mama. The ice cream truck is coming down our street. Can I have some money for ice cream?"

"How many times do I have to tell you I don't have money for ice cream, Marilyn? Not in my purse, not anywhere. Do you understand?"

"But you have candy bars, Mama. Why can't I have ice cream?"

"Marilyn, get out of my room and leave me alone. I have a headache and I need quiet." Covering her eyes with her right arm, Mama slumped into her bed and sighed loudly.

"Mama?" I whispered as I placed my hand on her arm, "Are we poor?"

She didn't answer, so I tiptoed out of her bedroom disappointed over not getting my ice cream and sad for my mother who was always sick because we were poor. I was sure that's why she screamed at me so much.

"Poor people don't get ice cream," I whispered to myself. "They just get screamed at!"

Back outside, I sat on the concrete step with my dog, Inky, and tried to think of ways to get money for ice cream. "Santa lied to me, Inky." I remembered how last Christmas I'd told Santa I did not deserve a present. I told him how I wanted Mama to be happy and was sure a present would help. Santa told me what a good girl I was to think of my mother and promised he would give her a present which would make her happy. But he didn't, and now I vowed never to trust Santa again.

"Inky, what are we gonna do?" I turned my precious terrier around so I could look straight into her eyes. "You're my only friend, Inky." She licked my face and wagged her tail in happy agreement. "We need money," I said as I hugged her. "We need lots of money."

As my mind wandered, I remembered what Daddy had once told me as he put money into a blind man's cup. He said it was "Christian" to help the unfortunate. I didn't know what unfortunate meant, but I supposed it meant to be blind. And I didn't know what Christian meant either, but Daddy looked pleased when he said it. Suddenly, I knew how I was going to get the money.

My body tingled with anticipation as I tiptoed past Mama's bedroom and burst into the room my sister and I shared.

"Janine!" I whispered, shaking her sleeping body by the shoulders. "Wake up! We're gonna get money so we can have ice cream."

"Go way," she mumbled, blue eyes heavy with sleep.

"I said you get up! I need you to be blind. Here's your shoes, put them on. I gotta get a cup. You close your eyes and I'll sing. People will give us money and we can get ice cream!" Hot blood rushed to my face as I visualized my cup full of money.

Dodging sharp tumbleweeds made Janine cry. Her pouty mouth and lack of willingness made me angry.

"You're gonna play blind so we won't be poor!" I insisted, pulling her by one arm. "Now shut your eyes until I tell you to open them."

No one answered the first door I knocked on, so I led my "blind" sister to the next. This time, the door swung open.

"Yes? Can I help you?" This white-haired woman had a kind face. I was sure she would want to be Christian!

"My sister is blind and I can sing. Do you want to hear me sing 'Onward Christian Soldiers'?" Adrenaline was pulsating throughout my tiny body, and I notice my voice sounded higher than usual.

"Aren't you the new preacher's girls?" quizzed the old lady. "Isn't your father Pastor Morston?" Her face began to look crinkled and not as nice.

"Mama says I can sing good and Daddy says it's Christian to give money to the blind." I boldly held out my cup.

"Well, I guess a dime won't break me...but does your mother know what you two are doing?" The old lady's voice sounded like she was scolding us, but she *did* put a shiny dime in my cup.

"Thank you, Ma'am! God bless you!" I jerked my sister towards the street and headed for the next house.

We had successfully covered two streets before I heard Mama's familiar shrill. "Marilyn Joyce Morston! Come here this minute!" She stormed towards us from up the street, her face contorted with anger. She grabbed my upper arm, digging her fingernails into my flesh. "How dare you humiliate me like this? How dare – "

"But Mama, I have money, see?" I shook the cup, hoping the sound of rattling coins might calm her down. "We're not poor anymore!" Apparently she was not impressed. The pain of her fingernails made me walk on tiptoes as my mother trotted me home with Janine trailing behind nervously sucking her two middle fingers.

"How dare you, you bad girl!" Mama spewed through clenched teeth, trying to look as if nothing was wrong for the sake of the neighbors. "We've only been here one month and now everyone in the neighborhood thinks we're beggars – or worse, that we ask our kids to beg *for* us! I'll teach you never to pull this stunt again," she hissed.

Once inside the house, Mama crouched like some wild beast and began screaming strange words I knew were not very nice. Her voice was high and fierce, bouncing off the walls and charging the air with angry vibrations. With one violent rip, my clothes were pulled from my frozen body and I was knocked hard against the piano. For a moment or two, I thought I was suffocating.

Mama grabbed me by my hair and everything seemed to go in slow motion. I felt the coldness of the bathtub on my naked body and the paralyzing sting of the razor-thin belt. A small voice began screaming promises never to do it again. My heart sank as I suddenly realized Daddy wouldn't be there to see me die.

Then, sounding like a record turning too slowly, I heard Mama's crying voice. "See what you made me do, you bad girl? You made me do it again."

Time passed slowly. I felt myself returning to life through intermittent phases of dank darkness and painful light. As time dragged on, the powerful sensations of physical pain and emotional despair returned with a vengeance. In this darkened state, alienated from all human

12

warmth, I felt no will to try to overcome them, and time mercifully held me suspended in my paralysis. I abandoned myself freely to my helplessness and yielded to the coldness around me.

Then, in the distance, I heard the squeak of the back-door screen and a thud as it banged shut. The ceiling of the bathroom slowly came into focus. It was darker in the room than I remembered. I could hear the sound of a man's approaching footsteps, then nothing. A mustached face appeared above me, staring down in total disbelief.

"Daddy?" I cried helplessly, "Is that you, Daddy?"

Horrified, he stared at my naked, blood-splattered body. Then with robotic movements, he leaned down, lifted me into his arms and headed for the sink.

"Daddy, it's my fault...I made her mad...I always make her mad. I try to make her happy, b-b-but I make her mad...It's not her fault, Daddy. I'm the one who's bad!" My body convulsed with sobs as my eyes searched Daddy's face for the slightest reaction.

There was none.

"I ruined your church belt, Daddy. It's all red and dirty now."

Still no reaction. Instead, he calmly washed my body, covered the cuts with Mercurochrome and bandaged them with the skill of a trained medic. As he worked, I could hear him talking to himself real low so no one could hear.

"Even animals – even dumb animals – protect their young," he muttered angrily.

3 - TURN THE OTHER CHEEK

I never heard Daddy talk about how God called him to preach. Only my mother talked of his "calling" – how Daddy tried to fight it, but God slammed all the doors shut until he had no choice but to preach. I always thought it very odd that God would want someone He had to force to be a preacher.

I was nine when my father achieved my mother's dream of a full-time ministry. Daddy was ordained and we moved to a small town nestled in the New Mexico Mountains to live in the parsonage next to the small church. Unfortunately, many of the parishioners felt it was their duty to keep their pastor poor so he wouldn't be tempted with the sin of pride.

New Mexico dust storms were fierce, and every time they blew, our curtains stood out from the windows until they were horizontal to the ceiling. We tried to plug the large gaps between the windowpanes and the wall with chewing gum, but without much success. Janine and I slept with pots between us when it rained so our bed would not get soaked. Mouse droppings in our silverware drawer were common and cockroaches rampant. No one in the congregation lived as poorly as we did.

Since Daddy got paid once a month, Mama's child-hood experiences during the Depression came in handy. One of her favorite meals was what she called a "New England Boiled Dinner": one head of cabbage, four potatoes, four carrots, one onion, and one ham hock – all boiled for one hour. She made me cook the cornbread.

The only thing that saved us during the days remaining after Daddy's paltry salary was exhausted was the charge account at the local grocery store. To my delight, I learned that my stash of candy could be replenished whenever I ran low. But my inexhaustible supply was threatened when Daddy discovered, to his horror, that he owed more than his entire monthly check.

Janine's and my eating habits were atrocious. Since Mama was never up before breakfast, we would raid the icebox where a batch of Daddy's fudge or divinity was always available. The results of these breakfasts were prominently displayed on my bulging body. By the time I entered third grade I had a serious eating disorder and was addicted to chocolate. I was beginning to understand why Mama used chocolate to "feel better" and, like her, I began stashing it. My stash made me feel powerful in some perverse way. It was my very own "secret weapon" with which to cope.

In spite of my obesity, I entered the third grade thinking I was someone special – the daughter of the town's spiritual shepherd. But this didn't last. Taunts and jeers about my weight produced a new coldness inside me. Even when I charged candy at the grocery store, friends were around only as long as the candy lasted. To make matters worse, because corporal punishment was the norm, my teacher kept me literally tied to my chair most of the time. While Janine had learned to express herself with tears, my release was hyper kinesis – a virtually unknown condition in 1953. The other kids made fun, calling me a "caged monkey" and I felt the hardness in me solidify further with each jeer.

To make matters worse, Daddy, finding it easier to cope with Janine's finger sucking and tears than with my more aggressive expression, began to openly favor her. She was always either in his lap sucking her fingers and holding her blanket, or snuggled up next to him in bed. And any time an argument ensued, I could bet my candy stash Daddy would take her side and I would get punished for "being mean to her." She learned very quickly to scream before I ever touched her, so I decided early on if I was going to get a whipping for hitting her, I was at least going to get the satisfaction of hitting her first. Mama made matters worse by comparing us constantly. Naturally, I always came out on the short end of that comparison. I was learning I was the bad girl and Janine was the good girl. Not only did they believe it, I began to believe it, too.

Mama's isolation had sadly retarded my social skills. By keeping me busy so I wouldn't "get in trouble" she had actually increased the possibility of my not "keeping up appearances" which were so important to her. She made sure every minute of my day was filled with chores no nine-year-old girl should have to do, including the family ironing. If one wrinkle was in a white shirt, she made me dampen the entire batch of ironing and do it all over again. If one spoon was not up to her specifications, she made me rewash every dish, glass, pot, and all silverware in the cupboard again. I had no friends because I had no time to make friends and no social skills to use.

It was this social immaturity which led to my mistake of teasing Rosie. It was no big deal, really. Seeing Rosie talking to a boy on the playground one day, I sang, "Rosie has a boyfriend." Rosie was three years older than the other third graders and she found her self-esteem in gang leadership. She had a sixth sense about victims, and she saw I was fair game. On the way home from school that day, she and her friends trapped me under the sewage bridge and beat me up royally.

When I finally got home and told Daddy what had happened, he said I was to "turn the other cheek" like the Bible says. "OK, now I know what the game rules are," I thought, and I went to school the next morning feeling it was God-honoring not to fight. Miss Rose, our principal, had different ideas. She called me into her office, asked me if Rosie had caused all the bruises on my face, and I said yes. She asked me if I defended myself: did I fight back? I told her my Daddy said I was to "turn the other cheek," to which she responded, "Hogwash. Either you fight back or I'll use the paddle on you." When I told Daddy what Miss Rose had said, he said it was none of her business since it happened off the school grounds, after school was over. True to his passive nature, he repeated his admonishment to "turn the other cheek."

The next day Rosie and her gang got me under the sewage bridge again, and the following morning Miss Rose made me take down my blue jeans, lean over her desk, and take five hits from her thick paddle with the holes in it. Still, Daddy said not to fight back. For several weeks this scenario played daily until Rosie just got tired of beating me up. I wasn't a challenge to her anymore, and she just quit one day, out of the blue. I never talked to her again.

I finished the third grade friendless as usual, but the summer still held promise for fun and adventure. Daddy's vacation was coming up, and we would soon be heading for my favorite place in the whole world: Shabbona, Illinois, the place where Grandma Morston lived. I could hardly wait!

My parents were an odd pair: Daddy never wanted anyone to know how poor we were, and Mama never wanted us to *look poor*. However, she never passed up the opportunity to get a good deal by "poor-mouthing" to strangers. Now, four days into our hot trip to Illinois, they were fighting again. Daddy, still embarrassed by our half-price motel room Mama acquired by telling the clerk we were "just a poor preacher's family," had driven off and left her standing in the parking lot. She had picked the wrong time to demand her right to drive. The fighting would stop today because we would be pulling up in front of Grandma Morston's house and every one would act happy.

I was tired of jostling around in the hot car, and playing "billboard alphabet" with Janine. Sitting still for more than thirty minutes was torture for me.

"Janine! Are you ready for all the slobbering?" I teased my somber-faced sister.

"I won't let her slobber on me," she asserted.

"Ooh, sloppy kisses all over your face, Janine. Grandma will do it! Slobber, slobber, mushy, mushy!"

Even though we teased about Grandma's kisses and all the fuss she made over us, we secretly relished the idea of someone making such a show out of seeing us again. It had been three years since we had seen Grandma and Grandpa, so we had grown quite a bit.

"Comb your hair, Marilyn," snapped Mama, "and make sure your face is clean. I don't want Grandma thinking I'm not a good mother. Janine, get those fingers out of your mouth. Do you want Grandma thinking you're still a baby?

Seven years old is too old to be sucking your fingers."
Mother was trying to draw on her eyebrows with her pencil
while she talked, and the bumpy road made her miss the
mark.

"Cal, could you drive a little smoother, please? I
can't put on my eyebrows if you're going to drive so herky-
jerky."

"It's a good thing you're not driving, Elise. We could
all be killed just so you could have some eyebrows."
Daddy's attempt at humor didn't please Mama, but Janine
and I thought it was a riot!

"Tell that one to Grandma, Daddy! She'll laugh,
too!" I said, trying to be included in the humor.

"You keep your big mouth shut!" Mama demanded.
She never turned around, but glared at me through her mirror
as she worked on her eyebrows.

"I was talking to Daddy," I sulked. "You always answer for Daddy." I moved my legs over and sat up real tall in
the back seat so Mama couldn't see me in her mirror.

"I can hardly wait for Grandma's molasses cookies!"
I whispered to Janine.

"That's all you ever think about is food," Janine said
woodenly. "That's why you're so fat."

"And you're Jack in the beanstalk, skinny bones. You
look like a skeleton: the neck bone's connected to the
shoulder bone..." I sang with unabashed pleasure as I made
faces and insulting gestures.

"Daddy, Marilyn's making fun of me," whined
Janine as the tears began to flow. "Make her stop, Daddy."

Daddy reached backwards to hit me, but I moved and
he missed, making the car jerk to the right. "Marilyn, if you
make me stop this car, you'll be sorry! Leave your sister
alone, or I'll stop the car!"

"You always take her side! She started it, not me!" I complained as I glared at Janine and secretly vowed to get even when Daddy wasn't around to protect his little baby.

There it was: the white, wood-paneled, two-story house with green shutters and porches, surrounded by gardens of flowers. As Daddy turned down the familiar driveway and honked the horn, my skin broke out in goose bumps. I decided I would be the last one out of the car. That way my hugs and kisses would last the longest.

I laughed as I watched Grandma squeal with delight, smothering everyone else with wet kisses and warm, firm hugs. Finally, I jumped out of the car, running into Grandma's arms.

"Look, Grandma: I've grown!" I chattered nervously.

"Oh, sweet Jesus, you surely have!" Grandma said as she held me at arm's length to have a good look. Her eyes were shiny with tears of joy and her spectacles were all spotty. Her eyes crinkled as she looked me over from head to foot. "Child, you have your father's hazel eyes and the Morston chin. You get prettier every time I see you!" she said as she stroked my sun-streaked hair and looked at me with too much love. It made me uncomfortable.

"Do you have molasses cookies, Grandma?" I asked, trying to change the subject. Actually, I knew Grandma always had molasses cookies hidden in the cellar.

"Of course I do, but first we'll eat supper. Let me get Tink. He's been waiting all day to see you girls." Grandma turned to go up the stairs when her eyes landed on my arms. "Marilyn, what happened here?" she asked as she pointed to the bruises on my arms.

I nervously glanced at Mama before stammering, "Uh-I-I fell off my bike, Grandma. I was hurt real bad, but now I'm OK. Can we eat now, Grandma?"

Grandma looked first at Mama, then at Daddy. Neither uttered a word.

I was ravenous by the time everyone sat down at the kitchen table. The feast set before us was too wonderful for words: chicken-fried steaks, mashed potatoes and milk gravy, fried okra, cornbread, pickled cucumbers, green onions, green beans, and slices of the biggest, reddest tomatoes I had ever seen. Grandma gave each of us a huge, frosty glass of fresh milk and then sat down to hear her son offer thanks to her God.

Once I started eating, I just couldn't stop. I felt drugged, but I kept eating. Despite my mother's glares, I asked for more chocolate meringue pie. I knew she wouldn't slap me in front of Grandma.

When the meal was over, Mama went upstairs to take a nap, Janine went outside to catch fireflies, and Daddy went in the parlor to argue politics with his brothers. I helped Grandma do the dishes.

"Grandma, how come you have a boy's name?" I asked as I stacked the plates. "Frankie is a boy's name."

"It's short for Frances, and once Tink started calling me Frankie, everyone did." Grandma seemed so contented in her kitchen—not like Mama who hated being in the kitchen. Grandma softly sang to herself as she lovingly cleaned each dish. Her voice was a soothing balm to my hyper nerves and I joined in on the part of the hymns that I knew. My favorite was "I Must Tell Jesus" because it said what I had felt inside so often.

"Grandma, do you tell Jesus everything?"

"Oh, yes, Marilyn, everything."

"How do you know Jesus hears you?"

Grandma smiled at my inquisitive nature. "His Word says He hears all our problems, all our cares, all our secret desires. You talk to Him, don't you, Marilyn?" Grandma's voice sounded like a warbling bird song. It had to be the kindest, most beautiful sound in the world.

"I talk to Him, but I don't know if He hears me," I muttered. "I even got baptized for Him, but I don't know if He hears me 'cause He never talks to me. Do you ever *hear* Him, Grandma?"

"He talks to me in here," Grandma said as she clutched her chest.

"You hear him in your chest?" I was amazed to know Grandma's chest had ears. "What's He sound like?"

"I feel Him in my heart. I *hear* Him in my mind. He sounds like an important thought in my mind." The soft way Grandma looked right into my soul made me uncomfortable. It felt like she knew all my thoughts and feelings, and it scared me.

Grandma had started rubbing my back with soft, loving strokes as she talked. No one but Grandma ever touched me with so much tenderness. Part of me soaked up her soft touches; but another part felt very uncomfortable with all this intimacy, so I moved away and continued chattering.

"Grandma, how come I got only one Grandma and Grandpa? Every one's supposed to have two, aren't they?"

"You had a Grandpa Charlie, but he died about four years ago. And your Grandma Foale died of cancer when your mother was just a teenager. She was a school teacher, I hear."

"Did my other Grandpa work for the railroad, too?"

"Oh, no, child. He was an educated man. Sure was a shame the way he lost his fortune in the Depression. Used to be a very wealthy salesman, I hear. He was a talker, that one. Both your Grandpas were mighty stubborn men, Marilyn, arguing 'til they was blue in the face."

"What did they argue about?"

"Everything and nothing. Charlie died a lonely old

man. When they found his body, it was in a room stacked with newspapers from years done passed. What a mess." Grandma clicked her tongue as she led me up the stairs to the bedrooms.

"Well, you go to sleep now and when you wake up I'll fix you biscuits and gravy with your bacon and eggs. A growing girl needs plenty of good food in her stomach."

"What time do you get up? Eight?" I wanted to keep the conversation going so Grandma wouldn't leave the room. No one ever took the time to talk to me like Grandma did, and no one else seemed as interested in what I said.

"Eight? Oh my, child! By eight I'll already have the wash on the line and pies in the oven!" she said as she kissed me goodnight and turned to leave the room.

Unwilling to let her leave, I sat up in the bed and asked, "Do you use a washboard, Grandma? I know how to use a washboard, and I can help you!"

"Why would I need a washboard? My wringer washer gets my clothes clean and the sun makes them white."

"Mama says washing machines don't get the clothes clean enough. I wash all our clothes on the washboard. I scrub each one real hard with P&G Soap and Pine Sol. Then I rinse 'em, ring 'em out, put 'em in a basket, and Mama takes 'em to the wash-o-mat to wash 'em again. Then…" I gulped for air, "I hang 'em on the line, wait for 'em to dry, take 'em down, sprinkle 'em with water from the Pepsi bottle, fold 'em up and put 'em in a plastic bag in the icebox. Then…" I gulped again, "I iron 'em and hang 'em up. I iron perfect, too! Not one wrinkle in any shirt! It has to be perfect or I have to sprinkle all of 'em over again and start all over. The ironing has to be perfect for Mama! I'm a real good ironer, Grandma!" I bragged, jutting out my cleft chin.

"You do all the ironing, even Calvin's white shirts?" Grandma seemed to be having difficulty believing that a nine-year-old child could do all the ironing.

"I swear to God, Grandma! All of it!"

"Don't swear to God, child. Let your yes be yes and your no be no, like the Word says." Grandma looked stern, but not mad. "Why do you have to do all the washing and ironing? Don't your Ma do the housework?"

"Nope. I do. When I'm at school I come home on my lunch hour and dust all the furniture – especially the piano – so it'll look shiny for Mama's piano pupils. I sweep, too. Then, after school I do the dishes and scrub the kitchen floor and the back porch. It smells from Inky's puppies. Then I help Daddy cook supper."

"Calvin does the cooking? Well, he always did enjoy watching me cook. Maybe he picked up some how-to's along the way." Grandma was thinking hard now, I could tell. "If your Ma doesn't do any chores, what does she do to stay busy?" Grandma had a puzzled look on her face.

"She's sick a lot, and she takes naps. She gets mad if you wake her up, too. Brrruther, let me tell you, you never wake up Mama, if you know what's good for you!" I was on a roll, but all of a sudden, I realized how much I was telling. "Don't tell anyone what I told you, OK, Grandma? I'll get in trouble if you tell anyone." I knew I had broken the silence rule, and I was scared enough to start covering my tracks. "She sells cards and calendars to make extra money 'cause we're poor, so she gets tired a lot. Don't tell anyone, OK?"

"Oh, shush. There's no dishonor in being poor, Marilyn. Our Savior was poor, too. There's only dishonor in being dishonest...or *lazy*..." Grandma was looking like her thoughts were far off, and she closed her eyes like she was praying. "Do you know you have angels watching over you?" she asked with her eyes still closed.

"Really? I haven't seen any of them. How do you know they're there?"

"Every night before I get into bed, I kneel and ask God to send His angels to watch over you and protect my girls – especially you, Marilyn."

"Why?"

"Something inside tells me you need angels – more than the others," she whispered to herself, but I heard what she said. "Marilyn, do you have any friends?"

"I don't need friends, Grandma. Besides, I don't have time to play. I have to work hard so the church people will like us. If they don't like us we'll have to move again. Everything has to be perfect, Grandma. Daddy could get voted out of the church, Mama says, if the people don't like us."

"No friends? Aren't there friends at church for you to play with?"

"Mama says I talk too much so she doesn't want me being friends with any of the church kids. Do you think I talk too much, Grandma?" My eyes were glued to Grandma's face as I waited for her affirmation.

"Well, you're just a child. A body has to expect a child to talk sometimes. Don't you have anyone to talk to?" Grandma looked concerned.

"Sure I do! I have a dog and her name is Inky! She just had puppies again, and boy, was Mama ever mad at her!" I was secretly pleased at the thought of Inky defying my mother's wishes.

"Just don't seem right for a child not to have any friends. We're only young once and a child your age should be playing outside in the fresh air with friends her own age." Grandma seemed to be fussing to herself when Janine entered the room.

"Come one, Janine. Climb up here with your sister." She said as she helped Janine into bed. There wouldn't be any more private talks with Grandma now that my sister was in the room.

"Good night, girls. Grandma leaned over the bed and gave each of us a wet goodnight kiss before she turned out the light. As she closed the door, I felt that familiar loneliness again, and I felt afraid of all the secrets I had told Grandma.

~~~

Eyes aflame with hellish evil, the female beast growled at me and lunged forward. I felt my heart stop and leave my head to do the pumping of my blood. I tried to run, but something kept me frozen to the tree branch. I tried to scream, but no sound escaped. Inside my head, where no one could hear, an explosion of terror ripped through my brain. Claws...gnarly hands...somebody save me...falling...falling... f-a-l-l-l

In cowering docility I waited for the fatal impact. My heart began to beat again and the sound drowned out the explosion in my brain. My lungs screamed for oxygen, but none came. Suspended in terror, I opened my eyes for one last look. The sweat in my eyes made it difficult to see Grandma's guestroom.

It was that same nightmare again: fresh and full of impact. I lay in the darkness listening to my disconnected breathing, wishing I could get into bed with Grandma and tell her about my nightmare like Janine did with Daddy.

It was 1954 and it seemed to me that everyone was talking about building bomb shelters. Rock and Roll was causing quite a stir, and old "I LIKE IKE" buttons were still hanging on Mama and Daddy's dresser. New Mexico was a Democratic State and Daddy was one of the few Republicans who admitted they were Republicans.

This was Daddy's second year at this church, and already there was talk of building a new sanctuary with lots of classrooms. Mama had outdone herself in this full-time ministry. The people appreciated her musical abilities as well as her ability to get things done. There were duets, trios, quartets, all-girl-sextets, instrumental groups, and any other type of special music one could imagine. The church members felt Mama was "doing them proud," and she loved all the attention she was getting.

Janine and I usually seemed to be in trouble for giggling in church, and Mama always sat on the back pew during Daddy's sermons. From that vantage point she could scrutinize not only our behavior, but also the behavior of the entire congregation. She noticed who slept during the sermon, who seemed to be under conviction, who wasn't in church that day, and other helpful information which would always be given to Daddy over Sunday Dinner.

Mother coughed when we giggled or whispered, coughed when Daddy's sermon was running over-time, and coughed when Daddy made another grammatical error. Her coughing gave us ample material to fuel the laughter, especially after she recruited us into her trio. Mother thought of it as job security to show the congregation how talented the pastor's family was.

After the hymns, the announcements, the offertory, and the Doxology, Janine and I knew it was ShowTime for us. It was called "special music," of course, and wasn't supposed to show any similarity to show business, but it always seemed like show biz to me. Janine and I would watch Mother rise from her piano bench, and, like Leonard Bernstein posturing before the New York Philharmonic, she'd walk, music in hand, to center stage. My sister and I would obediently follow from the choir loft.

Janine and I would watch in humorous amazement as Mother's demeanor and posture metamorphosed into that of an opera singer: squared shoulders, tucked pelvis, her ample chest pushed forward, hands held together in front, chin up.

Janine, who sang alto, would stand on Mother's left. I, who sang the tenor part an octave higher than it was written, would stand on Mother's right. We knew to wait for Mother to pull herself up to her full 5'9" height, take a deep breath, and give a cursory glance over the congregation.

Then, as she would look left to cue the substitute pianist, Janine's eyes and mine would meet, but quickly look away lest we fall into laughter. A hush would fall over the congregation and after pausing just long enough to let the poignancy of the moment settle in, Mother would open her eyes wide, set her mouth with a pleasant professional half-smile, and lift her chin even higher to suggest the utmost in classical decorum. That's when it would happen.

Janine and I, able to see each other peripherally, would fall helplessly into giggling, which would earn each of us an immediate painful pinch behind the pulpit where no one could see. Mother's pinches were always painful enough to modify our behavior, and once we composed ourselves, the show would go on.

Once we were safely seated in our middle pew, however, the scenario would be replayed during Daddy's sermon as we whispered, giggled, imitated Mother, and ignored her incessant coughing from the back pew.

I think the church members must have thought Mother had tuberculosis.

I'm sure no one knew how important laughter was to me. With all of the inconsistencies between my "perfectly happy" public life and my abusive home life, I took every opportunity to act out in a public setting. I knew her Patrician upbringing, and her need for the appearance of perfection would ensure my safety in church; however, it was as though I was always sitting on the jagged edge of the pew – waiting for the inevitable. The tension was so great inside me, I had to either laugh or go completely insane.

~~~

In the summer before the fourth grade, I finally got a friend. We met at church and something just clicked between us. Her name was Patricia Sue Taft, and she was eight months older than I, so she was going into the fifth grade. Patty had long red hair, big jade-green eyes, and a body I would have loved to have myself. Mama wasn't too crazy about my new friend from the start. Her father was a new convert who used to drink, her mother was in a mental institution, and Patty had the nerve to wear short-shorts and go to movies.

Patty taught me to love horseback riding, and climbing mountains. Together, we read every Nancy Drew book published, waited for the Library Van on Saturday, and built our own happy reality through books.

The best thing about Patty was that she never laughed at me like the other kids did, for being fat. She encouraged me constantly, telling me she'd trade her body for my beautiful face any day of the week. She knew what it was to live with pain at home, and she just accepted me as I was, period. I, in turn, gave her the courage to be more daring: to reach beyond her grasp. She went along with all of my schemes, and we had too much fun to think about our problems. She was a gift from God: a friend born for such a horrifying time as was coming.

~~~

My parents were effectively building up the congregation, and one of the reasons was their love of young people. One of their favorite places to take all of us was the skating rink that was ten miles away. I looked forward to these outings because when they were having fun, my parents didn't argue. Though they didn't believe in dancing, they were Fred and Ginger on roller skates. They looked like two teenagers in love, fitting together like two pieces of a puzzle. It was wonderful watching them laugh and tease each other in front of everyone. Even at ten, I could feel the sparks of passion being ignited between them. For days, after a skating party, Daddy would touch Mama in intimate touches, and she'd respond with hugs and kisses. Our bedroom was next to the kitchen, and I'd hear them talking to each other late at night, like they liked each other. Patty said when they talked like that, it meant they had just made love.

~~~

Mama made frequent trips to El Paso to shop for her clothes. She said it was the only way she could relieve tension. Unfortunately, she had to take us with her. I hated being with her on these shopping marathons as much as she hated having me with her. She could never make up her mind about what she bought, which meant several trips back and forth between the same stores, taking back what she had just bought, then doubting her decision to take it back. Once Mama got into her shopping state of mind, she forgot all about us. If she hadn't been hypoglycemic, we never would have been given anything to eat, so shopping, for me, was torture.

Once, when I was six, I got lost in the middle of downtown El Paso, and Mama didn't notice I was missing for hours. I stood in the middle of the sidewalk and cried until I threw up, but still no Mama. It was dusk when the policemen found her, and then I got punished for "running off." It was because of that whipping that coat hangers became scarce in our house. Janine and I hid them daily, preferring to be slapped or pinched.

Now that I was ten, I didn't follow Mama around the stores anymore. I preferred to wait for her in the park that had alligators swimming in a concrete pond. The "Alligator Park" was always full of people, and my favorite past-time was studying each passerby. Living with Mama's erratic behavior had made it necessary to become proficient in body language, and I employed it during my people-watching times in the park. Instinctively, I knew how each passerby was feeling, and I'd try to figure out why. It was as if I felt each person's pain as deeply as if it were my own. I desperately wanted to fix whatever was wrong.

Mama hated the way I "stared" at people, and she slapped me every time she caught me. Only Patty understood what I was looking for in the faces of strangers.

Patty and I learned if we shared each other's chores, they got done faster and were more fun. We liked working at her house better than working at mine. Mama was such a perfectionist we couldn't please her. If one soap suds was on a glass, she'd make us do all of the dishes over again; if one wrinkle was in a shirt – even at the bottom – she'd make me dampen all of the clothes again, and iron them again. It was, she thought, the perfect way to teach me excellent work habits. Patty thought my mother was crazier than her mother.

~~~

We always wondered what the funny smell was that came out of the bathroom whenever Daddy was in there. One day I was feeling particularly bold and I told Patty we were going to peek through the crack in the bathroom door and find out what was making that smell. My boldness was always appealing to Patty, but peeking through Pastor Morston's bathroom door seemed a little radical to her. As usual, though, my enthusiasm won her over and she peeked through the crack. There sat her pastor on the toilet with a cigarette in his hand! Then I took a peek, and, sure enough, there was Daddy smoking in the bathroom! This was a big time discovery for both of us, especially in view of what was going on at the church concerning Rheba Roberts.

Rheba was a very pretty lady at church who wanted to teach teenagers in the Sunday School class. But several of the older ladies had objected to her being a teacher because they suspected that she smoked. They had never actually seen her smoking, but they smelled it on her clothes and hair. I wondered if the women were telling the whole truth. I thought they were just jealous of Rheba's looks because their own husbands couldn't keep their eyes off her. She was a sexy redhead who looked like Rita Hayworth. One thing I knew for sure: Mama did not like Rheba Roberts!

With all the hubbub over smoking, I thought it was just about the worst sin in the world, and I convinced Patty to go on a "Nancy Drew" mission to catch this lady with a cigarette in her hand. Once she was caught, I would take our eyewitness information to Daddy, who would, of course, greatly appreciate our spy work. But it didn't turn out as planned.

When I told Daddy what we had done, he reacted like a mad man. For the first time in my life, I received a vicious, skin-tearing belt lashing from not Mama, but Daddy!

Now, peeking through the crack in the bathroom door, I thought I finally understood why Daddy had reacted so badly: he was a smoker, too!

But it would be much later when I would understand what really happened that day between Daddy and me. Until then, I would see less and less of him as he distanced himself from his nosey daughter.

6 - GOD, WHY HAVE YOU FORSAKEN ME?

It was 11:00 p.m., July 25, 1956 when it happened: a night neither Janine nor I would ever forget. We were preparing for bed and Janine was in the bathroom. The New Mexico winds were howling, "Freckles" was nursing her pups in the screened-in back porch, and Mama was banging "Beer Barrel Polka" on the piano in the front of the house. She was angry Daddy had gone to Albuquerque for a five-day convention.

I was in our bedroom, in the back of the house, and had just removed my blouse when I heard it: a growl unlike any Freckles had ever made, but more like a deranged man or a large caged animal. Immediately my eyes darted towards the window by the back porch. That window always bothered me because anyone could stand on the back porch and see right into our bedroom. I thought I saw a face, but my fear made me doubt what I saw. Then I heard it again: a low-voiced moan followed by cursing groans. Then banging that suggested someone was falling against the porch banisters. Moving closer to the window, I squinted out into the dark to see if I was imagining someone was out there. Once before, I had seen a face in the window and Mama had convinced me it was "all in my head."

Before I knew what happened, a horrible face pressed itself against the window, causing me to freeze in terror. My brain went as numb as my body, and, unable to move or think, I stood staring at the face in the window as I heard Freckles begin vicious barking. I heard banging on the screen door and window. My heart was beating so loud I had trouble hearing the commotion until the last thud, followed by eight screaming puppies and one vicious spaniel.

I never would have moved if it had not been for Janine who, hearing the noises and seeing my frozen white face, grabbed my arm and pulled me out into the kitchen.

Lost in her music, Mama didn't hear Janine's screams; but once I shook my paralysis and became hysterical, Mama stopped and listened.

Three hysterical females crashed through the front door, heading for Penny's Cafe where Sheriff Churney and Police Chief Norfork spent their days and nights waiting for some crime to liven up their small town. All that stood between the parsonage and Penny's Cafe was a railroad track and two fields of goat heads: those hard-needled thorns that caused even horses to limp once they were embedded between their hooves.

I never felt one of those goat heads as I ran bare-footed across the fields. I had long ago learned to shut off all physical feeling. Unaware of my bleeding feet, I was the first to crash through the door at the cafe, and it seemed an eternity before either man understood what I was screaming.

All these law enforcers had to do was walk across the railroad track to search the parsonage, but our town was so crime-free that they rarely ever got to use their lights and sirens. Each man got into his respective official car, turned on the sirens and lights, drove one block down to the railroad crossing, then one block back to the parsonage. It was their finest hour and they intended to make it last as long as possible.

It did not surprise me that no one was found either in the yard or in the parsonage. I resented the men's suspicious eyes and condescending voices as they hypothesized that it had only been the harmless wino "Ramon" who lived behind the parsonage. They figured he had a "snout full" and just wandered into the wrong house, falling on the puppies. They found him sitting in his outhouse "drunker than a skunk" and oblivious to the rest of the world, so they got in their official cars and left us alone in the house as they drove back to Penny's Cafe where their coffee hadn't had time to cool.

My sister and I were terrified, as Mama left us alone in the house, explaining she was going down to the Churchfield's to "borrow a gun for our protection." Our tearful pleas to go with her fell on deaf ears, and only thirty minutes after the terrifying incident, Mama walked out of the house leaving ten-year-old Janine and twelve-year-old me alone in our terror.

Huddled together under an end table by the couch, we clutched each other for comfort. Both of us, now hypersensitive, heard scary noises amplified throughout the house.

"Are you scared, Janine?" I whispered. There was no doubt in my mind that the intruder would return and kill us, so I didn't want to tip him off to our location by whispering too loud.

"Mama should have let us go with her," Janine whispered. "She shouldn't have left us here all alone."

"Maybe we should pray, Janine." My mind raced through all the possible remedies for our situation, but Janine didn't think praying would do any good.

"If Jesus could stand right here where we could see Him, then that would be ok. But I've never seen Him. I bet He isn't even real!" Janine asserted.

"Grandma says she prays for guardian angels for me. Maybe they're here and we just can't see them." I comforted myself with the thought.

"You'll believe anything, won't you?" Janine snapped. "Our mother doesn't care about us at all or she never would've left us all alone tonight." Janine's big blue eyes grew stone cold as she spoke and her face had hatred covering it like gauze.

"I'm really scared, Janine," I whispered as I tried to

35

move closer to her. Just yesterday I had placed myself between her and Mama, preferring to take the beating she was getting with the broom handle. She had told me last night that what I did was "not logical," but I thought she probably was glad I had done it. Now, under the table, Janine put her arm around my shoulders in a way that let me know she was protecting me. She was definitely braver than I was!

"If Daddy was here, he'd never leave us alone," she whispered, trying to comfort me. "Daddy would never let me stay in this house alone."

"Daddy might protect you, Janine, but he wouldn't protect me. When Rosie was beating me up every day, did he protect me? And when Lupita stuck me with pins, did he protect me?"

"Who's Lupita?"

"You don't remember her 'cause you were just a baby. She used to be our babysitter and she stuck me with needles because I told Mama how she brought men in after Mama left. Daddy never believed me, even when I showed him the holes she made in my arm."

"Because you lie so much, Marilyn." My sister's attitude had returned and she removed her arm from my shoulders.

"No, he just likes you better. I have to do all the work while you run off to your friends' houses to have fun," I argued.

"Well, I'm not going to let Mama ruin my life! I'm going to be a majorette and I'm going to college! Then I can get out of this dump and have a real life." Janine spoke with absolute resolve. "I'll show her I'm not retarded!"

"Show who? Who thinks you're retarded?" I asked, slightly dazed.

"Mama thinks I'm retarded. I heard her talking to Mrs. Dobson. She thought I was asleep, but I wasn't, and she

36

showed the horses I drew to Mrs. Dobson. She asked her if she thought I was retarded because my horses didn't look like horses. She thinks she's so smart just because she used to be an artist. She had no right to show my horses to anyone. They're private. They're my horses." Janine's voice broke and her eyes began to tear; but she quickly recovered and announced it was time for us to go to sleep.

The panic that had crescendoed in dreadful waves suddenly departed, leaving in its wake an empty numbness that allowed us to drift off into troubled sleep, still clutching each other under the end table.

Fourteen hundred miles away, in the darkness of Shabbona, Grandma woke with a start. She got out of bed, fell to her knees, praying God would send extra guardian angels to protect her granddaughters in New Mexico. She stayed on her knees until morning, singing hymn after hymn, not knowing why she couldn't sleep.

~~~

Two years later, in September of 1958, I was thrilled to be entering High School. Patty and I walked two miles uphill the first morning, discussing how life would be different for me as a high school student. She was a sophomore, so she felt a responsibility to show me the ropes. All of her forewarning didn't prepare me for the walls lined with pimple-faced boys, jeans hung low on their hips, hair slicked back like James Dean, all making horrible kissing sounds as we walked by. I walked down the hall feeling fat, ugly, and out of place. My naiveté glared like sun on ice, and it gave the boys more pleasure than they deserved as they each tried to out-embarrass me. If Patty hadn't been beside me, I don't think I would have made it to class.

On the way home, we took our lunch money we had saved, bought tamales from the vendor who pushed his cart up and down the street, and then we went to Cathy's Cafe to dance to the music of Elvis, Buddy Holly, and Sam Cooke.

We got one song for one nickel, or six songs for a quarter, and we danced with each other until we couldn't breathe anymore.

By the time I was a freshman, I had been taking piano and voice lessons for long enough to know I had real talent. I had been singing in church since I was five, and my ear for harmony was extraordinarily good. Music was the only radiance that broke through my enshrouding darkness and made me feel beautiful. Mozart made me feel connected to beauty; hymns made me feel the presence of God; and rock and roll was just plain fun. My musical talent was my only source of self-esteem. The only time my parents seemed happy to have me around was when I "did them proud" by performing well.

Only Patty knew my secret: I was the only fourteen-year-old girl who had not yet become a woman. Other girls talked about their periods and I pretended to know what they were talking about, but I didn't. I thought I would never grow out of childhood – I'd always be a fat girl.

Usually I had vivid dreams every night. The first night after starting school I didn't dream at all. When I awoke I found I couldn't move any of my muscles without extreme pain. My throat felt like someone had forced a telephone pole down it, and my tongue was swollen and in unspeakable pain. As I opened my eyes, I noticed a woman sitting on my bed and, though she looked vaguely familiar, I couldn't remember who she was.

"Marilyn? Are you awake?" she asked cautiously.

I tried to speak, but my swollen, chewed-up tongue would not cooperate.

"You father almost had a heart attack trying to hold you down, Marilyn. You know what a strong man he is, but he just couldn't hold you down." The woman kept talking, but I couldn't make my brain focus on what was being said. I just stared at this woman and noticed how frightened her eyes looked.

"You've been asleep for two days, Marilyn. We tried to wake you up, but you just wouldn't respond. The doctor says you have to stay in bed and sleep so your brain cells can rebuild themselves." Her babbling was irritating me, and then she put her hand on her forehead, sighed loudly, and asked, "Oh dear, why did this have to happen to me?"

Who is this woman, and who is Marilyn? I wondered. I lay like a zombie, unable to move, think, or feel anything but total pain. Not only did I have no memory of high school – I had no memory of who I was or where I was. All I knew was that I hurt everywhere and I wanted to sleep.

Two days later, with some memory recovery, and able to drink liquids, I asked my mother what had happened to me.

"It's nothing serious, Marilyn. Just has to do with you not starting your periods yet. Once you start, the problem will be gone." Mama never looked me in the eye. I had heard Daddy say, over and over, "If a man won't look you straight in the eye when he talks to you, don't trust him," so I wasn't trusting Mama's story now. I knew something freaky was wrong, especially as Daddy continued to avoid eye contact with me.

Even when Mama drove me home from the big medical center in El Paso, she still insisted there was nothing seriously wrong with me. She gave me Dilantin pills to take three times a day, saying they would "calm me down so I could start my periods." The next week I had an EEG, and Mama still insisted nothing was wrong, though I heard her whispering to Daddy that night. Even after dozens of repeat episodes – and the ensuing recovery periods at home – Mama still insisted nothing was wrong. Daddy neither denied nor confirmed Mama's assertions, making himself even scarcer than before.

I was finding it more and more difficult to explain to my teachers why I was absent so much. When they would ask the nature of my illness, I'd tell them it was "my nerves." They did not react sympathetically to my explanations, and my grades began to plummet. Life was becoming complicated, and then one day it just fell apart.

It was just before Thanksgiving, about 3:00 Wednesday afternoon. I had been sitting in my secret hideaway: the peach tree where I hid and listened to Mama yell for me. It always amused me to hear her getting so frustrated when I didn't come running right away. Janine, though, had told me I'd better come in this time: something was up.

Mama sat on my bed as she started to explain about my problem. "Marilyn, your problem is not about periods. It's called 'epilepsy' and the doctors think you might have been brain damaged at birth. See," she continued as she put her hand on my arm without looking me in the eye, "your father was in the Service when you were born – it was war time, you know – and the doctor that was supposed to deliver you couldn't be there for me. So this real old doctor with bad eyesight delivered you. He used instruments to pull you out, and the doctors think he might have damaged your right temporal lobe in the process. What you've been having is called 'grand mal seizures: epilepsy.'"

I just sat: dumbfounded at first, words swirling around inside my head like an echo chant. My eyes searched her face for some meaning, but she just looked down at her lap. Immediately, I thought of the two people I knew who had this thing called "epilepsy": Dorothy, the daughter of the people that owned the five and dime store. She was forty years old, but acted like a five-year-old. Her gums were big and ugly, and I had always thought she needed to be sent to a mental hospital. Then there was Lynn: thirty-eight years old, who sat in the choir loft on Sundays, putting on her makeup and talking to herself. She carried dolls, and everyone said she would never be older than eight years old because she was mentally retarded. She, too, was facially disfigured, and her body odor was offensive to my nostrils. Not knowing anyone with epilepsy who *wasn't* *also* *retarded*, I automatically assumed the two handicaps were the same. Now I knew, for sure, that I was a freak.

Anger rose within me as I realized how long my own mother had been lying to me. She, who whipped me mercilessly for lying, had been lying to me for months. And now that I had finally accepted her explanation for my seizures, she was pulling the rug out from under me by telling me she had been lying to me all along. I hated her for lying, I hated her for not looking me in the eye when she finally told me the truth, and I hated myself for being such a freak.

"Marilyn, you cannot tell anyone you have epilepsy, do you understand? Not even your blabber-mouthed friend, Patty!" Mama shook me to make her point. Now she was looking me in the eye. "No one can ever know about your problem. Some people think epilepsy is demon-possession. Boy," she said, releasing me, "there are those who could have a field day with this! They'd love to run your father out of the church by spreading it around that Satan possesses his daughter! This has to be our secret; do you hear me, Marilyn?"

Mama lectured on, but I wasn't listening. The possibility that I was demon-possessed scared me into paralysis. All I could think about was something I had heard my father say in a sermon: TO BE ABSENT FROM THE BODY IS TO BE PRESENT WITH THE LORD.

Later that night, I was home alone. My parents were somewhere playing dominoes and Janine was at a friend's house practicing her baton twirling. Only my dog Freckles and I were in the house. As I watched Freckles sleep, the pressure in my mind began to boil out of control: like a pressurized cauldron gurgling with poisonous malevolence, it boiled over until I could stand the heat no longer. Devoid of reason or thought control, I picked up the heavy broom handle and walked towards my beloved Freckles. It was as if I was watching someone else do to Freckles what my mother had done to me. In that moment, I made the transformation from victim to persecutor of the trusting, innocent love of my life. I didn't plan it, I didn't want it, and I never dreamt I would do it: it just happened and I couldn't control it.

Lying on the floor by my precious Freckles, I froze, glassy-eyed, in a catatonic state of despair. All I wanted was to be absent from the body: to die with Freckles.

Freckles died three months later. She had a heart attack while chasing a car; but there was no doubt in my mind that it was the beating that killed her. Engulfed in my guilt, I spent each night begging God to forgive me for hurting Freckles, but I never felt His forgiveness. I didn't expect to feel His forgiveness if I was demon-possessed. I prayed because I was scared.

As a small child, I had known Jesus as someone to please, and I did my best to please Him (and everyone else); but I knew I never did. Mama always told me I couldn't hide from God: He watched me all of the time, and saw every bad thing I did. I believed God cared more about the bad things I did than He did about who I was.

On Sunday afternoon Mama would make everyone in the house lie down and take a nap so she could have absolute quiet. Janine always left the house, but I spent the time in my room listening to Charles E. Fuller preach on the radio program "The Old Fashioned Revival Hour." I loved hearing how God "loved us while we were yet sinners." I knew I was a sinner! I desperately wanted to believe that God could love a freak like me, and I thought Charles E. Fuller could tell me how to get God to take all the bad stuff out of me; but my prayers were little more than pleadings of a victim. Charles E. Fuller promised that Jesus would always be there for me, but Jesus hadn't been there when I needed Him the most. He had allowed me to become not only an unwanted freak, but maybe even demon-possessed. I understood, all-too-well, the words of Jesus as He died on the cross: *My God, my God, why hast thou forsaken me?*

Each of my grade school teachers had maintained discipline in her own special way. They ranged from hickory switches on my legs, rulers on the back of my hand, tying me to the chair so I couldn't get up, and making me sit out in the hall all day. Later, I was told my seventh grade teacher had asked to have me placed in her class. She was an old maid who wore army-issued pumps, and something about her made me realize there would be no testing of this woman! She had watched me in the hall and realized I needed some stern, but non-abusive discipline. In her class I learned, for the first time, that discipline did not have to include abuse. I behaved very well in her class and made decent grades. Then I met Margaret Trouissant, my eighth grade teacher.

She was the most beautiful woman I had ever met: her blue-gray eyes were kind and alive, her gray hair had a white streak almost in the middle of her head, and her smile melted the stone wall around my heart. Her voice reminded me of Grandma's voice: melodic, soft as velvet, and hearing it made me feel instantly loved. With no children of her own, she adopted some of her students as her own and loved each of us unconditionally. She never had any behavioral problems in her class! I never wanted to please anyone so much in my life.

Margaret constantly affirmed me. When I would tell her a story she knew wasn't true, she'd tell me, with a twinkle in her eye, that I was the best storyteller she ever heard – not a "liar," but a "storyteller!" It was quite a switch from hearing at home how I brought shame to the family because I was such a liar! All of my life I had heard how humiliated my parents were each time they went to PTA meetings and heard my teachers' reports. They loved talking to Janine's teachers because she was so good, but I made them ashamed to be my parents.

Margaret recognized my talent for writing right away. She encouraged me to write poetry, ballads, and short stories. When she found out how talented I was musically, she encouraged me to write songs, which I did constantly. She'd stay at her desk after school and I'd hang around to talk to her as long as she'd let me. She laughed at my stories, told me how "delightful" I was, and built my self-esteem in myriad ways all during that year. I loved her more than I ever loved anyone except Grandma, and I blossomed under her loving tutelage. She had such a positive perspective on life: something that was totally foreign to me, and I soaked it up like a dried-out sponge. She gave me hope for the first time, and she gave it at a crucial turning point in my life.

I had been experiencing high fevers for several years, and always there was the same hallucination: I could feel the flesh falling away from the bones of my fingers, and felt bone rubbing bone as I rubbed my fingers together. My screams would bring my parents running with cold towels for my forehead, aspirin, and cold baths – anything that would bring down the fever. The same parents that had unceremoniously ignored me for so long were now there to fill my needs – but only if I was helpless and ill. Now, in addition to "acting out," I was discovering another way to get their attention. Having Margaret's positive attention provided some badly needed balance as I was learning negative ways to get attention at home.

To my surprise, Margaret was my English teacher in my sophomore year! Once again, she showed appreciation for my vivid imagination, even encouraging me to join the Balladeer's Club. It was an after-school club of students who wrote ballads from New Mexico folklore and then traveled to women's clubs to perform. With so much practice performing in church, I was a natural, and the other club members elected me as their president for three consecutive years.

Between the Balladeers Club and the Honors Chorale, I kept busy most of my high school years as a performer. But always in the background was Margaret: encouraging, hugging, delighting in me, and giving me courage. She made my sophomore year a turning point in my life. For the first time, I believed I could possibly be as special as Margaret said I was.

I didn't even mind that Mama was always there to share the credit with me when I received applause. I was just happy to finally be doing something right—something that didn't bring shame to my parents.

By this time, the Dilantin had my nocturnal grand mal seizures under control. I was now having them only when I was under extreme stress, and still only while I slept. I had done some reading on epilepsy and knew I was not demon-possessed. I was grateful I was experiencing seizures only when I was asleep. No one but my parents and Janine had witnessed my seizures.

My reputation as a perfect ironer had allowed me to earn extra money for several years, and it was while I was ironing in a customer's home that it happened.

It started with a feeling of uneasiness: like someone was staring at me, making me feel extremely self-conscious. In what seemed like hours, but was in reality only seconds, the feeling escalated to a feeling of paranoia that paralyzed me. To the outside observer it seemed nothing was happening except that I had stopped dragging the iron across the board. But inside, all hell was breaking loose. All the eyes on earth and in hell gawked at me as I tried to run, but their stares held me hostage. So disoriented I didn't know where I was, I was conscious only of staring eyes waiting to destroy me as I tried unsuccessfully to breathe. The pressure inside my mind fed on itself, squaring like an algebraic equation, until I thought I would self-destruct. My eyes darted left and right like those of a trapped animal, and I could feel my mouth curving into an insane half-smile that made me look like I was either demon-possessed or mentally ill. I tried to scream, but no sound escaped my lips. *God, is this how you treat your children?*

Then it came: a high pitched scream loaded with such emotional dynamite it terrified every one in the house. I could not have controlled it if my life had depended upon it.

"My God!" shouted the customer's husband, "Has she gone completely crazy?"

Hearing his comment, I broke into hysterical laughter and explained I was thinking of a joke I had heard and it was so funny I couldn't stop laughing.

"Well, if it's such a gut-buster, let's hear it," he challenged.

My keen survival instincts and my quick wit saved me from total humiliation that day, as it would in the future. But once again, I thought I was demon-possessed. I did not know I had just experienced my first psychomotor petit mal seizure.

Neither of my parents understood epilepsy. Not many people did in 1959. Most people thought it was a combination of mental illness and demon-possession. Daddy coped with this new embarrassment by going fishing more often. Mama coped with it by locking me in the closet while she gave piano lessons in the front room.

Sitting in the dark closet, sometimes sharing the space with mice, my anger began to seethe. I resented being punished for something I couldn't control. Not only was I the family outcast, I was also banned from the outside world. I watched Janine snuggle up to Daddy, still crawling into his bed at twelve years of age, still sucking her fingers like a baby, and I hated her for stealing Daddy's love away from me.

In what I later understood to be a symbolic way of taking back what had been stolen from me, I began to steal anything I could get my hands on. When church members had us over for Sunday dinner, I stole them blind, and it mattered not who the victim was, or even if I got caught. Rarely did I ever keep any of the booty. My high came from the risk involved in stealing, not in what I stole.

Daddy caught me stealing several times, but no matter how much he punished me, I kept on taking what did not belong to me. He found it almost impossible to control my behavior, and I, in return, became more rebellious. My personality was turning into barbed wire, and it angered Daddy that I was not more compliant like Janine. His frustration drove him to spend more time with Janine, even sharing his frustrations and feelings with her as one would do with a friend – or a wife.

Eventually, through experimentation with various drugs, my petit mal seizures were controlled to the extent that they occurred only during the pre-menstrual three days. Still fat, I concentrated on developing my musical abilities. I auditioned for, and won, a position in the New Mexico All State Choir. My reputation as an excellent singer, entertaining pianist, and composer of "shoobop" songs gave me some badly needed self confidence. Privately, I journalized my secret pain in the form of poetry, which was written under the pen name of "April." The names I gave my poems said it all: "I Wanted a Fairy Tale," "Feed The Child," "Suicide of a Stranger," "Epitaph of a Messiah," and "Two Faces Have I."

I'd binge on chocolate as I wrote my poems, lost in my own world at fifteen. Being fat was humiliating, but not as threatening to me as being thin and risking intimacy – at least my fat protected me from risking rejection for reasons other than obesity. Then I met Paul Horton.

Paul was two years older than I, and was a senior. He was President of the Chess Club, intelligent, and like me, had never had a relationship with someone of the opposite sex. He lived alone with his very possessive mother who had come to America from Germany. Paul did not have a strong male identity and he wasn't very good looking. But he had the ability to look beyond the obvious to the inner qualities of a person, and evidently he liked who he saw in me.

Paul was an excellent marksman and he took me with him when he went to the desert for target practice. His mother always came along to watch this female who was stealing her son's affections, but I didn't mind. I was just happy to finally have a real boyfriend. And I was thrilled to have another opportunity to learn something that would impress my father. He loved to hunt and I wanted to go with him – just the two of us.

Also, I started smoking, thinking that if Daddy knew I smoked, he would be more willing to take me on one of his hunting trips and not stay away from me so he could smoke in private.

Once before, Mama had pressured Daddy to take me off her hands, and he had begrudgingly taken me fishing with him. But he had left the tent early in the morning and hadn't returned until twilight. I had spent the day picking flowers and trying to make the tent look like home for him, but he never noticed. After that, I reasoned that Daddy didn't need another daughter: he had Janine for that. What he needed was a son who could do "manly" things with him, so I learned to throw knives, ride motorcycles, ride horses, and became a decent archer. Still, he summarily avoided me unless I was out of control or sick. He never did take me hunting.

Having a real live boyfriend gave me some hope as a female, even though Mama advised me, "Protect your face. It's all you'll ever have. It's a cinch you'll never have a decent body." I tried to diet, but unable to keep the bingeing under control, I did the only thing I could think of: I began purging after every binge. By the end of my sophomore year,

48

I was fifty-three pounds lighter and so malnourished that I had to make daily visits to Dr. Woodrow's office for liver shots and Vitamin B. But I was slim and beautiful – everyone said so. Even my own father was bragging about how good I looked. And boys who had ignored me were now flocking to my doorstep. For the first time in my life, I knew what it felt like to have personal power: feminine sexual power and I exploited it without shame. I rolled it round on my tongue, savored every precious bite of it, and breathed it in like a long-overdue holiday. I was intoxicated with this new power, never thinking about its addictive powers. I was willing to be addicted forever, if that's what it took to feel this powerful!

8 - SAID THE SPIDER TO THE FLIES

By the time I was a junior, I had a reputation for stealing boyfriends and "going steady" with several boys at one time. The other girls called me "The Black Widow," and when a new boy would show interest in me he would be warned of my "web" by several of my peers. One of the "flies" that flew into my web was named Jimmy.

Patty and I were at the skating rink when I saw Jimmy and it was love at first sight for me. It consumed me, drove me, and controlled every waking thought. Jimmy was the proverbial tall, dark, and handsome man, with soft brown eyes and curly black hair. He was a twenty-year-old "man of the world" from Ohio who was just passing through with his buddy Ron. He decided to stick around when he met me. The attraction between us was so strong that even my absent father sat up and took notice. When I brought Jimmy to church and then home for hot chocolate, Daddy and he communicated without words. Jimmy knew he had better not defile this preacher's daughter! I ached to be defiled by him.

I spent every waking moment preoccupied with Jimmy, even spending my lunch hour in a phone booth at school talking to him. For the first time in my life I wanted to give away my precious virginity; but Jimmy always stopped the passion-fests before we went "all the way." Every date ended with me begging him to take me, and him sending me inside at great personal sacrifice. Though frustrated, I saw his self-discipline as the ultimate proof of his love for me. He wasn't anything like Mama had told me all men were.

By this time, I had learned not to take Mama seriously. She had lied to me too many times, and she had used me too many times to do what she should have been doing. I wasn't about to be her house slave now! And I had learned from her how to get my own way. Sixteen years of living with inconsistent rules and unpredictable consequences had left me without any respect for her opinions, warnings, or threats. By the time I met Jimmy, I had the ability to talk her into any scheme imaginable. At the age of thirty-seven, she was still little more than a child, herself, with erratic emotions and very little maturity. I, like Mama, was becoming self-absorbed and driven by my own needs.

Jimmy made me feel emotions I never knew I had. I was hooked on the sexual feelings, but I was even more hooked on the feeling of being needed. Finding out Jimmy had a drinking problem only fed my need to fix his problem. In 1960 I had never heard of "co-dependency," but I was smack dab in the middle of it with Jimmy. I had watched my mother fix Daddy's faults, and had watched Daddy passively assent to being fixed. I honestly believed women were created to civilize and fix men, and there was no doubt in my mind that my love could fix anything that was wrong with Jimmy. I would help him stop drinking, and I'd change him into someone my father would be proud to accept as his son-in-law. I was willing to become his wife and move to Ohio with him. There was only one small problem: he already had a wife in Ohio.

Sitting beside me in the theater on a Saturday after-noon, Jimmy told me how he had gotten a girl pregnant when he was sixteen, married her because he had to, but hadn't lived with her after the marriage. That's why he had left Ohio: to get away from his legal wife and child support. I was devastated, but quickly recovered to fix the problem. Jimmy would have to go back to Ohio, face divorce court and possible jail time for non-support. He could get a job and pay his back support, find an apartment, and then send for me. Jimmy left for Ohio shortly after that, promising to take care of all his problems.

After Jimmy left, I knew I had to tell Daddy about Jimmy's wife even though it meant facing his implacable anger. I assumed he would be impressed with Jimmy's return to Ohio to divorce his wife and pay child support. I thought he, too, would see it as proof of Jimmy's love for me. I was wrong.

This father who had ignored my needs unless it was a medical emergency, suddenly turned into a one-man vigilante force to protect his daughter's virginity. He called the sheriff and police chief to report a possible statutory rape and then intercepted Jimmy's mail and phone calls. Not to be stolen from again – and certainly not to be outdone – I rerouted Jimmy's calls to Patty's house, along with his mail. I made secret plans with Jimmy to run away, and I talked Patty into hitchhiking with me. But, out of all the New Mexico drivers, it was Daddy who stopped to pick us up.

I was confined to the house for a month, but still received mail from Jimmy which Patty brought to the house. Daddy went through my drawers and found the mail, and after he talked to Patty's father, that avenue of communication was closed down. Fortunately, I had been corresponding with Jimmy's sister, so it was easy enough to receive letters from someone named "Norma."

Once again, plans to run away were made and the time would coincide with the trip my parents were planning. Janine and I stayed with Patty for the two nights they were gone, and, again, Patty was talked into running away with me. This time we would drive Daddy's Dodge, and I made sure I had the extra set of keys before he and Mama left. Our plans were a cinch, we thought. But we had not counted on Janine's interference. Acting out of protectiveness of Daddy's car, Janine stole the keys and hid them, unbeknown to Patty and me. After searching for the keys, I asked a friend to hotwire the car; but even that failed. I never got to Ohio, and Jimmy eventually became discouraged enough to. stop trying to contact me.

Embittered, but unwilling to mourn yet another loss, I reconstructed my web and resumed fly catching. Juggling several steadies at a time kept me on my toes, but I was comfortable with chaos. Crisis management was my specialty, so I actually enjoyed living on the edge: waiting for one of the boyfriends to find out he wasn't the only steady in my life. My games were successful until I met Keith Paycock.

Keith moved to New Mexico in the middle of the school year, and he soon became the star quarterback on our football team. He was extremely good-looking, musically talented, and, at seventeen, he knew that God had called him to a special ministry of music and preaching. He refused to be scheduled into my date book: he demanded all of my attention, and for a while he got what he wanted.

We sang beautifully together. We had the awards to prove how good we were. Naturally, Mama was thrilled to have such a musically talented prospect for a son-in-law. Daddy approved of this fine Christian preacher boy for obvious reasons. They both thought Keith would get Jimmy out of my system.

Like my mother, Keith's mother gave piano lessons to support her two sons. Daddy let her use the church annex for her lessons. It was because of my sister that we found out what a con artist Mrs. Paycock was. Janine told Mama how Mrs. Paycock would spend the entire hour of her piano lesson trying to find out what food we had in our refrigerator. She tried to manipulate Janine into sneaking food to her, but Janine would not be manipulated – not by Mama, and certainly not by this obnoxious, obese stranger!

Embarrassed by his mother, Keith compensated for it by trying to fix me. Controlling behavior was familiar to me, so I tolerated his attempts at first. I knew every girl in high school wanted to be his steady, so I tolerated his controlling personality out of personal pride.

Every morning at 7:00, Keith would be at my house for morning devotions before we faced a "day of temptation by the enemy," as Keith so eloquently put it. We would read the scriptures, and then Keith would hold my hand and pray for me. I had never had anyone pray with me and for me, and I liked the idea of someone petitioning God on my behalf. But I thought Keith's interpretation of the scriptures was extremely legalistic. I had been listening to Charles E. Fuller long enough to know about grace, and Keith didn't seem to know what it was, much less how to extend it. I soon grew tired of Keith correcting me every time I said "darn" and I was sick of his sermons every time I said "heck." I had been thin – and powerful – long enough to recognize some personal choices and Keith was definitely cramping my style!

One night Keith drove Mama and me to see a play at the college that was ten miles away. I had his senior ring hanging around my neck. After the play was over, I noticed one of the actors motioning for me to come to him up on the stage. Flattered that he had noticed me out of hundreds of others, I walked up the stage to see what he wanted. His name was Warren, and he wanted me to be his date at the cast party. I informed Mama and Keith I would not be going home with them. Mama objected at first, but as usual, I was able to talk her into letting me stay in the city with this good looking stranger. Keith never said a word. He lust looked at me in total disbelief. He and Mama drove the ten miles home in utter silence.

By the time I was seventeen, I knew what I wanted to do with my life. I wanted to go to New York and make it big on Broadway. I met Marilyn Sizemore at the military hospital where Patty and I were candy stripers. Marilyn was also a great singer and she wanted to use her talent to get out of her abusive home life. She convinced me we could make it big together, but first, she said, we had to get a wardrobe and money to live on. Marilyn was also an expert at shoplifting.

The two of us would-be-stars heisted merchandise from the best stores. Because we traveled all over New Mexico singing at competitions, we had access to better merchandise than would be sold in our small railroad track town. I told my parents the new clothes belonged to Marilyn, and she told her parents they belonged to me. It was the first time in my life that I was able to wear clothes that were not used, donated by church members, or hand-sewn by one of the kind old ladies in the church. At seventeen, I was in style and I loved every delicious moment of it. Still bingeing and purging, I had been thin for more than two years, and I looked good. I felt alive with sensuality.

While in Albuquerque at the All State Choir Recital, I took some medication to stay awake, and after three nights with no sleep I flipped out. Right in the middle of the choral and orchestral performance I fainted, and when I woke up I was in the hospital. Keith Paycock, though no longer my boyfriend, told the ambulance driver he was my husband and they let him ride to the hospital with me. When I awoke he was sitting by my bed. He told me that I had screamed for 45 minutes: before the ambulance got to the school, all the way to the hospital, and even in the emergency room. He said I didn't stop screaming until they gave me a shot. Then he told me that Daddy was driving 250 miles to take me home because the bus driver refused to let me ride on his bus.

And, true to form, Daddy did drive to Albuquerque to rescue his oldest daughter. It was, after all, a medical emergency.

~~~

Keith left town with his mother after she milked the church members for all she could get. She decided it would be more profitable to move on to new territory. I didn't miss him at all. I had boyfriends to spare, and eventually I narrowed them down to two. One of them was Clinton Furrow. He lived close by and was also a preacher's kid. His mother, like mine, was subject to fits of rage, and she used whatever she could get her hands on to keep all eight of her children in line. Even the sheriff was afraid of her after she shot at him. All he was trying to do was serve legal papers on her property. Everyone knew Mrs. Furrow – or "Mrs. Fury," as everyone called her – beat her kids with television cable wire and heavy iron skillets. She was only five feet tall, but she was an Arkansas tornado on wheels.

Mrs. Furrow made it very clear to Clinton, right from the start that she disapproved of me. For one thing, I was in the wrong denomination. For another, she had heard what a wild girl I was. She never would have believed that at seventeen, I was still a virgin. In retrospect, I see that she saw in me what she was in her teenage years: a sexually desirable, but controlling female. She had invested too much in her son to see it all thrown away because of his hormones!

Clinton was definitely nice to look at. Half-Irish, half-Cherokee, his dark features and high cheekbones gave him a debonair look. Tall and well built, he looked great in his football suit. He was gifted musically, both with his voice and his cello. As a child he played cello in the symphony, right along with fifty-year-old musicians. He was also well known for his deep bass singing voice, which he used to entertain students in the popular "shoobop" songs of the fifties. He was a libidinous seventeen-year-old who knew what he wanted to do with his life: make it big in the music world. No one doubted he would receive full scholarships to any university he chose.

But, like me, Clinton had been abused all his life. He was next to the youngest of the eight children that lived (she gave birth to sixteen, but only eight lived), and in addition to the beatings he received from his enraged mother, he also got picked on by his older siblings. The feelings he had for his mother were a combination of anger, hatred, and a need to please her. He had a real, but unacknowledged problem with controlling women: they were to be hunted and destroyed. Besides the strong sexual attraction, what drew us to each other was our mutual pain. Both of us had been victimized, both of us had learned to persecute, and both of us preacher's kids wanted to get as far away from home as possible.

Clinton's kisses were consuming and commanding, and I loved the drama of being possessed by this passionate male. What we didn't know about intimacy, we made up for in passion. Both of us loved living on the edge, and one Friday in October, two virgins drove to Mexico in order to assert their independence and, also, to be able to have intercourse without incurring the wrath of God. Two angry preacher's kids became man and wife, at least in the eyes of Mexico.

I would rue the day I ran away from home with Clinton Furrow.

~~~

Three days after our quickie Mexican wedding, still virgins, we told our parents. Having no money for a motel room, we had tried to consummate our vows in the back seat of Clinton's '57 Chevy Bel Air; but the farmer who owned the field ran us off with his shotgun. We drove home feeling frustrated, but secretly independent of our parents.

Mrs. Furrow threatened to annul the marriage, as did Daddy; but when I lied, saying we had consummated the marriage, Mama stepped in to fix the problem. Fearing what the church members would say about their preacher's daughter not having a religious ceremony, she suggested a fake wedding with Daddy performing the ceremony. Naturally, there would be photographers there to take pictures for the newspapers. Mrs. Furrow thought the whole idea was ridiculous, but Clinton appealed to her maternal instincts and she agreed to participate in the "hypocritical" ceremony. I was having second thoughts about being married, so when Mrs. Furrow agreed to the ceremony, I was disappointed. Two weeks later, however, when she changed her mind and threatened to annul the marriage and then tell everyone what a whore I was, it became a matter of principle with me. She would not win this war!

Mama changed the plan. Clinton and I would have our ceremony in El Paso, 150 miles away. The day before, she took me shopping for an inexpensive wedding dress that would photograph well. I talked her into buying two pairs of silk panties that had lace pockets sewn on them. It was the first time I remember Mama ever buying anything pretty for me.

The wedding went as planned, without a marriage certificate. It was staged by Mama to cover up the disgrace I had, once again, brought to the family. A photographer took pictures that were promptly sent to all of the newspapers. Just as there had been four people at my parents' wedding twenty years before, there were four people at our ceremony.

And just as my parents had spent their honeymoon night in the home of Mama's mother-in-law, we spent ours in the home of my unhappy mother-in-law. We had no money for a motel room, and the spare bedroom in my parents' home had been filled with newspapers for nine years.

The night I lost my virginity in Mrs. Furrow's home, I had three grand mal seizures. It was a preview of things to come.

~~~

Because he had a wife to support, but had no high school diploma, Clinton joined the Air Force, planning to continue his education while serving his country. I would continue living with my parents and stay in school. My husband would send for me after he finished boot camp and was settled in a permanent place. Mrs. Furrow caused such a stink over the "dishonesty" of our ceremony that Daddy accepted a church in El Paso just to get away from all the turmoil. Just before we moved to El Paso, I tied up one loose end: a boy I was still going steady with, or so he thought.

When Clinton and I decided to elope it was an impulsive decision made just fifteen minutes before we left for Mexico. Clinton didn't know it, but I still had the class ring of another boyfriend who was 200 miles away at military school. Les Moiré's mother had placed him in military school as a freshman when she married her new husband who was heir to the city newspaper. Her new husband was in the final stages of alcoholism, and she knew it would not be long before she took over his inheritance. She didn't want Les messing up her chances of becoming a rich and powerful woman, so she sent him to military school while she promptly had two children with her new husband.

It had been easy to have two boyfriends since Les was away at school most of the time. But now he was coming home for Thanksgiving, unaware that his girlfriend had married someone while he was away. I knew I had to be the one to tell him; it was only fair he hear it from me. So on his first night home, I told him of my marriage and gave back his ring.

Les was a total opposite of Clinton: passive and undemanding. He wished me good luck and drove back to military school without ever visiting his mother. I would not see him again for five years, and then it would be a life changing experience for both of us.

I was more sophisticated, I thought, than my unmarried high school peers. I felt valued and validated by my marital status. After all, a talented young man had just given up all his dreams of musical celebrity to marry me. I felt superior to all the other seniors who hadn't experienced the grownup validation of marriage. I went to my first dance: my senior prom. Daddy had a lot of do's and don'ts – mostly don'ts – and one of the biggest was no dancing, at least not with boys. Mama used to dance the Charleston in the parsonage, mostly to show us how well she could do the crossing of the knees part. And she played "worldly" songs at home. "Twelfth Street Rag" and "Beer Barrel Polka" were two of her favorites. We were allowed to listen to Elvis and all the other rock and roll artists, but we couldn't dance to them. I always wondered why it was a sin to jitterbug, but not such a sin to be in a parked car with a boy.

I served punch at the prom, but at least I was there. I felt a freedom then, like I no longer had to prove myself. When Clinton married me, it proved my value to everyone. Clinton and I looked good together, and because we had so much in common, everyone thought the marriage was made in heaven. The first two months of my senior year were the happiest ever. As a married woman, I no longer had to jump when Mama gave orders. For some reason, she respected the fact that I was now married and she changed her tactics accordingly.

Now, instead of screaming, threatening, and hitting, she began to manipulate in a "cutesy" way: like a childish coquette trying to win over her father. It was embarrassing and maddening to watch my mother turn into a child just to get her own way. I felt the dynamics changing before I got married, but afterwards the change was overtly obvious: she was the child and I was the adult. She would still have the last word, but now it sounded like a desperate child's tantrum.

For several years I had seen a pattern in Mama's behavior: first, she would find a needy person (usually an inadequate male), then she'd jump in to save him (or fix the problem), and then she'd expect undying gratitude from the person she had just "helped." If the helped one did not respond as Mama needed for him to respond, then she'd talk and act like she had been victimized. It wouldn't be too long after that she'd turn on the one she had helped, shaming him with his ingratitude "after all she'd done for him". The cycle was always the same: rescuer-helper, victim, and then persecutor.

The only one in the family who didn't seem to be sucked into Mama's cycle was Janine. Even as a young girl, she did not play Mama's game with her, and as a result, Mama dubbed her "the ungrateful -itch." The game Janine and Mama played was about control: Mama was frustrated because Janine, safe in the arms of Daddy, would not let Mama control her. My sister just ignored Mama's controlling ways.

For reasons I did not yet understand, I was unable to differentiate between Mama's needs and my needs. Even at five, when I asked Santa to bring her a gift instead of me, I was taking responsibility for Mama's obvious unhappiness. Eleven years later, I was still feeling compelled to make my mother happy: an impossible task since she was the consummate perfectionist.

The relationship between my father and her seemed to be non-existent, though I did not, at the time, know why. I just attributed it to Daddy's passive nature and Mama's need to control. I did notice that instead of being controlling in an aggressive way, she was now being controlling as a victim. I didn't know whose victim she was, but it was clear to me that someone either had victimized her, or was victimizing her. I felt both repulsion and anger when I was around her, which she sensed, so she began to try to make me happy. She sang all the current pop hits, loved Fats Domino, and talked about her days as a teenager. She told me how she had been sick after her mother died, missed her Senior year lying in bed, and how she had drawn all the art work for her yearbook while she was recovering. She began to try to be my friend – my teenage friend – and that angered me the most. She had given me reason to be angry, and his name was Ron Schneider.

~~~

Four years before, when I was thirteen, I was being hidden from the world lest people think my seizures were from demons. It was a time when I desperately needed my parents to tell me I was "ok," but was, instead, being reminded daily of "my problem." Mama, thirty-four at the time, had a seventeen-year-old musical protégé, Ron, who was living in the projects – government housing for the poor. Ron was sensitive, tall, and quite good looking. He played trumpet and Mama took him under her wing, so to speak. I'm sure his poverty had a lot to do with why Mama singled him out. She seemed to be attracted to the "less fortunate." She saw in them an opportunity to step in, rescue, and then remold them into her image. She was especially fond of "making preachers" out of young men.

It wasn't long before Ron started going everywhere we went, and what angered me the most was that she always let him sit in the passenger seat while Janine and I had to sit in the back. Naturally, I pointed out the unfairness of this arrangement numerous times. Each time I did, I would get pinched, glared at, or shoved in the back seat. I hated Ron Schneider. She treated him infinitely better than she ever treated her own daughters.

One summer day I was playing in the spring water of

the Gila National Forest where the four of us had driven. Ron and Mama were off somewhere by themselves, and Janine and I were left to amuse ourselves with nature. Janine, always the cynic, went looking for Mama and Ron. When she found them, they were lying on the grass kissing each other like long-time lovers.

When Janine told Daddy what she had seen, all hell broke loose in our house. The fights were tolerable: we had heard them for years. What was not tolerable was the sight I took in by accident. I had quietly sneaked out of bed to get some fudge when I heard sobbing sounds in the front room. I peeked around the doorframe and there was Daddy sitting on the floor, his head in Mama's lap, convulsing with gut-wrenching tears. I had seen my father cry only once before, and I hated my mother at that moment more than I had ever hated her for hurting me. I hated her for hurting Daddy, and I hated her for not acting her age. I hated her for being a hypocrite: preaching sexual morality to me while she was making out with a teenage boy. I think it was on that day that Janine and I both lost any vestige of respect we had left for Mama. In my idealism, I was positive I would never be like her. I was wrong.

~~~

Once Daddy moved us to El Paso in 1961 everything changed. The school was much larger and there were handsome senior boys all over the place. Patty's father had moved to El Paso just six months before, so Patty knew everyone. She introduced me to some of the most delicious looking boys I had ever seen. It was a smorgasbord of fantasy for me: an Epicurean delight to the girl who was still bingeing and purging. My dalliances with some of them helped cure my boredom and fill in the time until Clinton – off at boot camp – sent for me. Though I was never sexually unfaithful to Clinton, I was, indeed, disloyal to him. Mrs. Furrow, still trying to break up the marriage, wrote that she had seen me "doing it" in broad daylight, on a picnic table near her mountain home. I had never "done it" with anyone but Clinton, but I was sure flirting and fantasizing a lot in the new high school. My addiction to fantasy was in full swing, and I had more than enough actors in my off-Broadway production. The power I felt was intoxicating.

Somewhere deep inside, I knew I didn't want to be married to Clinton; but Mrs. Furrow's constant attempts to turn Clinton against me just made me more resolved that the old lady wouldn't win. Besides, Clinton was, at the moment, my only ticket out of my parents' home and life was getting harder there by the day.

In spite of my repulsion of Mama's teenage behavior, I found myself powerless as I tried to detach from her. There were no boundaries: no lines where she ended and I began. The emotional enmeshment between us was choking the life out of me and I felt I would suffocate if I didn't do something drastic. I had to survive!

I waited until I had received two allotment checks from the Air Force, and then one cold winter day I called one of the boys I had met in school and asked him to drive me to the airport. In the middle of a snowstorm, I left my parents' house without ever looking back or saying goodbye. I was going to Arkansas, where Clinton was permanently stationed, to be an independent adult.

~~~

Standing in the middle of the international airport, I felt lost and disoriented. I had never been away from home all by myself, and everything was so big and spread out it scared me. I had learned to be distrustful of strangers from my mother and now I was cognizant of all this money I was carrying with me. It was more money than I had ever seen in my life and I didn't want to lose it or, worse yet, have it stolen from me. I found the rest rooms and once I was inside my own stall, I stuffed the bills into the lace pockets of the silk panties Mama had bought me the day before my fake wedding.

It wasn't until I was sitting in the jet that I realized I had not notified Clinton that I was on my way to Arkansas. I knew he was still living on the base, so he wouldn't have an apartment ready for me. I was in such deep thought about my dilemma I didn't notice the man who sat down in the seat beside me.

"Hi," he said with a smile, "mind if I sit by you?" He sat down without waiting for my response. "My name is Ray and I'm going to Memphis. Where are you going?"

"What? Oh. I'm Marilyn and I'm going to Arkansas. My husband is waiting for me there." I added the part about my husband just in case this stranger had any strange ideas.

"Is this your first time away from home?" he asked in a sly voice. "I ask only because you look scared."

"Of course not!" I retorted. I didn't want him thinking I was unsophisticated. I changed the subject quickly. "Why are you going to Memphis, Ray?"

"I'm attending a psychiatric convention there."

"Oh, are you a patient?" My sardonic comment was an attempt to hide my insecurity, and he laughed with appreciation for my wit. The conversation that flowed from that point helped me relax on my first flight, and just as I was feeling some relief from my anxiety we heard a voice announcing we would be landing in Dallas because of engine problems.

I had never coped with change very well, and this time was no different. This was my first flight and I had no idea what this change meant. Where was I supposed to go when I got off the plane? What was I supposed to do? Did this mean I would never get to Arkansas? In a daze, I felt myself being pushed toward the door of the plane, and when I ended up inside the airport I couldn't breathe. My mind raced through a thousand thoughts as I stood in the middle of the airport, being buffeted by impatient travelers. I was a child again, lost in the Alligator Park in El Paso. Heart pounding and dizzy, I began to sweat profusely. Then I became mentally, emotionally, and physically paralyzed. Unable to think or move, I felt my legs getting weaker and I fought hard to keep from passing out. I didn't even feel his hand when Ray took hold of my arm.

I stared speechlessly at the hotel clerk as he asked if there would be one or two people occupying this room. I vaguely heard someone with a male voice say, "Two." As if hypnotized, I walked to the strange hotel room beside a stranger I barely knew. I don't remember entering the room or anything else about that night.

The next morning I opened my eyes and wondered where I was. Noticing the man asleep beside me, my heart sank as the shameful realization hit me: I was probably now an adulteress. My mouth went dry and it felt like cat hair was stuck in my throat. I wanted to puke, but I didn't have time. The walls moved like warped circus mirrors, and the floor wouldn't lie still for me. From deep in the center of my body came a nauseating heat that spread outward until my entire body was on fire. I felt all of the filth of the world on my conscience and I couldn't stand the burden. Afraid I'd wake the stranger, I crawled on the rolling floor to find my clothes and put them on inside out. I took the money out of the panty pockets and quietly exited the room. Once I found the registration desk, I stammered, "Would you tell my husband in room 306 that I have already paid my half of the room, please?"

I never looked the clerk in the eye as I handed him all the money I had: $523. But I did see his hand go into his pocket as he said, "Do you know your clothes are on inside out?" Then he laughed. I ran to the rest room thinking about the thirty pieces of silver Judas received and how he tried to give it back to absolve himself of his guilt. I barely made it to the stall before I puked.

~~~

When I finally arrived in Arkansas, it was 5:30 in the evening, and Clinton was delighted to see me, even if it was a surprise. At 7:00 that same evening we arrived at the home of Kenneth and Mim, friends from Louisiana that Clinton had known for two months. Before dinner was served Clinton suggested we play a card game. He, like I, had never been permitted to play cards, so he knew I didn't know any card games.

"This game is called '52 pickup' and you're it, Marilyn!" he announced. Then he threw the deck of cards on the floor, and in front of these people to whom I had just been introduced, he demanded that I pick up all the cards. I just looked at him in disbelief. I thought it was a joke, or else a very stupid game. When I didn't pick them up, he commanded me to do so as he grabbed me by my hair.

"You threw them down, so you pick them up!" I retorted, grabbing his hand. Clinton threw me on the floor, smashed my face into the cards, and commanded in an evil loud voice, "I said pick them up!"

Angry, yes; but even more, I was humiliated. I wrestled myself free from his hold and ran outside to get away from him. I had just arrived in the town two hours before, with no money, and I knew no one but Clinton. I had no where to go, so I had no options. I stood still until Clinton caught up to me and we walked until he found a cheap motel.

As we entered the room, before I could remove my coat, Clinton ripped all my clothes off and began pummeling me with his fists. He knocked me down, pinning me to the floor with his muscular legs and put his hands around my throat. His rage was out of control as he strangled me into unconsciousness.

The first sensation I was aware of when I regained

consciousness was unbearable pain inside my body. Clinton was so caught up in his violence he didn't notice I was awake. But he was screaming through clenched teeth, "How dare you make me look bad in front of my friends...Who do you think you are, you – " No obscenities were spared as rage suffused him, and I lay on the floor in passive docility as I was being raped. Except for the sex, it wasn't that different from what I had experienced at the hands of my mother. And it would not be the last time.

~~~

In our first year together Clinton and I fought constantly. He would, again, strangle me until I passed out, and then buy me donuts to say he was sorry. I would throw the donuts on the floor and smash them with my feet to express my unwillingness to forgive. His need for violent sex scared me and I began to believe all the horrible things Mama had told me about sex. I thought what I was experiencing was normal behavior for men. It didn't even seem strange to me that Clinton could pray such beautiful prayers in church and then come home and beat on me. It was what I had always known, and it seemed normal. I thought all Christians lived like that until Sue Howell told me different.

Bob and Sue Howell were godsends for me. They had been married two years, had a baby son, and were very active in the church Clinton and I attended. Bob was several years older than I, but Sue was three years older and we hit it off right away. They practiced true hospitality, and even if all they had in the refrigerator were eggs, Sue would cook us great scrambled eggs for dinner. They were well founded in biblical doctrine, fun to be with, and were always available when I needed someone to whom I could bare my soul. Clinton went hunting with Bob, and I would look through old picture albums with Sue and laugh at her childhood pictures. She taught me how to shop, cook, clean house, and be happy in the joy of the Lord.

Sue and Bob knew they were called to ministry, and one of the first things they did was put together a gospel team, complete with a traveling quartet and two preachers. Clinton's bass voice was a welcome asset, as was my piano playing. We began traveling on weekends all over Arkansas and surrounding states. We attended the all-night quartet convention in Memphis and Sue showed me the seat in the balcony where Elvis sat all alone as he listened to the quartets singing gospel songs. In 1962 gospel quartets were very popular in Christian circles, and we met them all.

In April of '62 I found out I was pregnant. My grand mal seizures escalated to three a week. Needing someone to be with me at all times, I asked Patty to come to Arkansas for seven months until the baby was born. Patty's presence in our home forced Clinton to control his violent outbursts – at least in front of Patty. Because I was constantly in a helpless state, recuperating from seizures, Clinton actually came through with some nurturing for me. He, like my parents, responded well to helplessness.

One month before the baby was due, the Air Force doctors told me I would never make it through labor with my female problems and seizures working against me. They decided a Caesarian section was the only way to deliver my baby. When Daddy heard how helpless I was, he told me to fly to El Paso and have the surgery in a civilian hospital, which the government would pay for because it was a "medical emergency." So, two weeks before I was due, I boarded a jet for El Paso to have my child. Clinton stayed in Arkansas.

Being back in my parents' home was, in a strange way, comforting for me. At least no one there would beat me up in my pregnant condition. But I was lonelier than ever in the strange hospital with no friends to visit me. And I was scared I would die with a seizure in my unconscious state.

In the delivery room I heard a nurse utter, "My God, we have a baby having a baby here!" and I felt ashamed of myself for not being more mature. Now sixty pounds heavier than I was nine months ago, I also felt ashamed of the way I looked, especially as word got out I was hospitalized and some of my old boyfriends started showing up.

Mama was working as a secretary at the time, but she visited me every single day, and I badly needed what nurturing she was able to give. After Mark was born Mama insisted that I train him – and any other children I might have – to call her "Nana." She informed me she never wanted to be called "Grandma." She was, she said, going to be thirty-nine for a long time, and she didn't want grandchildren giving away her age by calling her "Grandma." I knew Mama was childish, even obsessive about looking young, but I never thought she would be ashamed to be a grandmother! Just when I should have been the happiest, I felt like I had, once again, brought more shame and disgrace to my mother.

Clinton arrived in El Paso three weeks after Mark was born, and he wanted to show off his son to his own family in New Mexico. I wanted to show Mark, too, and I wanted to sleep in a real bed, even if it was Mrs. Furrow's bed. I had been recuperating on Mama's couch since her guest bedroom was filled with newspapers.

Mrs. Furrow was very proud of her grandson, but she still didn't like me at all. She found fault with everything I did, and she let me know of her displeasure. With stitches still in me from the navel down, I was in great pain. I asked Clinton to take the diapers to the laundry. His mother launched into a diatribe of insults, trying to shame me for not washing Mark's diapers in the bathtub as she always had. She shamed me for being so wasteful of her son's hard-earned money, saying only a lazy person would be so wasteful. She went through stories about all eight of her children, telling me what a hard life she had and what a trooper she was. It didn't seem to make any difference that she had her babies by normal childbirth, while I had stitches in me from surgery.

The stress of being in her home was too much for me and I had another grand mal seizure in my sleep. When I regained consciousness the next day, I could hear Mrs. Furrow ranting and raving about how her son had been betrayed.

"Even when you buy a horse, Clinton, you have the right to know if the horse is any good or not. Sure as shootin' you got a bum steer this time! If she had told you about her seizures you wouldn't have married her. Maybe we can sue her for not telling you what you were gettin' into."

I wondered why Clinton didn't tell his mother he had known about the seizures before we married. He acted like he was afraid of his mother, and it angered me. He seemed so subservient and ingratiating around her – totally different than he acted away from her. Even at eighteen, I understood that Clinton hated, but feared, his mother. I knew there was a definite connection between his beating of me and his hatred for his mother. He was totally emasculated by his controlling mother, and he took out his anger on me, trying to prove his masculinity through brute force. I understood all of this, but I had no control over it: no solution.

When Mark was four weeks old, we drove Mrs. Furrow's car back to Arkansas. I decided I wanted to go back to school and get my high school diploma, a decision that seemed to threaten Clinton. He wanted me home where no one could talk to me, and he certainly didn't want me getting more educated! I persevered, though, and found a baby sitter to watch Mark while I went to school. The school administrators were not thrilled about having me in their school. They thought I would be a bad influence on single girls, so they put very tight restrictions on me: no physical education classes, no social functions, and no discussing my personal life with any of the students. I felt like a wart, but I finished school.

The day before graduation Bob and Sue Howell left for Arizona, so they were not there to see me graduate. But Mark was, and even at eighteen months, he recognized his Mama in her robe. I was easy to spot: I was the only graduate who couldn't afford black pumps, and I was pregnant again.

I had planned to leave Clinton as soon as I had my diploma. His outbursts increased as I began to lose the weight I gained in my first pregnancy. Whenever a soldier would whistle at me, Clinton's insane jealousy would erupt and he'd start accusing me of playing around on him. Sometimes it would escalate into physical violence, and with his foot on my neck, he'd promise, "If it's the last thing I ever do, I'll see that you're locked away in a mental hospital so you can never see your son again."

Now, pregnant again, I felt trapped in my miserable marriage. I knew I couldn't afford to pay for another C-section, so I'd have to stay until this second baby was born.

When it was almost time to deliver, I received a visit from Daddy. By now, Daddy knew of Clinton's abuse and because I was, once again, helpless, he considered this a "medical emergency." He, himself, would drive me back to El Paso to have this second child.

I waited for Daddy all day, and finally, just as it was turning dark, I saw his car coming down the street. I picked up Mark and hurried outside to greet Daddy before he came inside. In a moment of protectiveness, Daddy held out his arms to hug me and I stood staring at him with a look of incredulity. I did not remember ever being hugged by Daddy in my twenty years of life. I had only a split moment to savor the delight of that embrace, but it became, in that tick of time, a treasure that would last long after Daddy's lifetime.

~~~

Serious complications made this delivery more difficult than the first one. Clinton was summoned and he arrived in El Paso just as John was being delivered. My parents look worried as he hurried into the operating room where the surgeon was waiting for him. Decisions had to be made: decisions that would be life changing for me, and as my husband, Clinton would make them. Without my consent or approval, Clinton decided that a Tubal Ligation would be performed on his twenty-year-old wife. I would never have another child.

The long drive back to Arkansas was unbearable, but I had no idea what was wrong with me. I just knew I wanted to die as soon as possible. Clinton had decided I wouldn't stay with my parents after this surgery. He didn't like the way Daddy looked at him, and he really got angry when Daddy told him he'd better be treating his grandsons right! So one week after my surgery, we were on the road back to Arkansas. Once again, Mrs. Furrow loaned her car to her son. She would fly to Arkansas and drive it back to New Mexico.

By the time we arrived in Arkansas, I had a fever of 106 degrees and was hallucinating badly. The last thing I remembered was sitting in a truck stop booth, rubbing my fingers together and feeling bone on bone.

I never arrived home, but was hospitalized in a military hospital immediately. For the next two weeks I lay unconscious as I was fed intravenously. My only memory was of leaving my body and hovering above it as I watched the doctors and medics trying to bring me back to life. I knew I was dying, and while I wanted to die, I didn't want to leave earth from a hospital room. I tried to scream that I was alive, but no one heard me. I heard the doctors pronounce me dead.

~~~

Fourteen hundred miles away, Grandma Morston, feeling troubled in her spirit, put down her broom and fell to her knees in prayer. She prayed, I heard, for over an hour, though she didn't know exactly what she was praying for, or for whom she was interceding.

~~~

I was in the hospital four weeks, and it was during my third week when I felt someone wiggling my toes. Too tired to open my eyes, I ignored the touch. Then I heard a wonderful masculine voice say, "Wake up, twinkle toes! It's time for you to come back into the land of the living!"

Slowly I opened my eyes, and there at the foot of my

bed was the most beautiful man I had ever seen. I though I must be in Heaven, and this man must be Gabriel dressed up in a white medic's uniform. He was too beautiful to be a human being. But he was, and his name was Reggie.

For the next two weeks Reggie gave me more love and nurturing than I ever knew existed. He woke me up every morning with his "twinkle toes" routine, bathed me, stroked my hair, told me how beautiful I was, and touched me with a gentleness that I had felt only from Grandma. He read to me, held my hand as he told me over and over what a "miracle" I was. He told me how I had died from an infection, but had been miraculously brought back to life. He said the whole hospital was talking about the miracle. He brought me flowers, candy, and numerous other gifts. He told me how wonderful life was, and how wonderful I was. He made me feel beautiful and treasured. He made me want to live again, and I wanted to live for Reggie.

Six weeks after John was born, I left the hospital. In my fight to live I had not yet held my newborn son, and I was desperately "in love" with someone who was not my son's father: someone who, like my father, was a medic; someone who had loved me while I was profoundly helpless.

~~~

The next ten months were a nightmare. The violence escalated again as I began to lose weight. Still faithfully attending church, I also was having an affair with Reggie. I knew what I was doing was not pleasing to God, but driven by all my unmet needs, I felt powerless to stop the relationship. The abuse I was receiving from Clinton only served to justify my affair. I knew Clinton would kill Reggie if he ever found out about our affair, but after tasting nurturing love from a man, I could not control my love-binge. I lived for my moments with Reggie, and Clinton's midnight shift provided me ample opportunity to indulge my needs.

One June night in 1965 Clinton was waiting as I quietly shut the door. He didn't usually wake up until 11:00 at night, but this night he had been awake since 9:00 and I was not home. Spewing out a string of obscenities, he demanded to know where I had been. And in some kind of insane defiance, I told him where I had been and what I had been doing.

His worst fears confirmed, Clinton now had nothing to lose. With both of his sons watching, he beat me until blood gushed from my face. Then he raped and sodomized me as Mark, his three year old son, screamed for him to stop. Lost in his insane rage, he then reached into the closet for his illegal sawed-off shotgun and loaded it. I wanted him to kill me, but he didn't. He picked up both of his sons, put his shoe on my neck, and spewed, "Say good-bye to your sons, Marilyn. It's the last time you'll ever see them alive." He left, slamming the door behind him.

I could have accepted my own death as punishment for my sins; but something fierce rose up within me at the thought of my innocent sons being killed. Ten minutes after I called the police, every law enforcement agency – both civil and military – was searching for Clinton. Helicopters noisily whirled overhead as my phone rang. I expected the caller to be another law enforcement officer, but it was Clinton.

"Mark," he said in a surreal monotone that sent chills up my back, "say good-bye to your mother." He kept trying to coerce Mark into saying good-bye, and it gave me time to hand the phone to the Colonel standing beside me.

~~~

I didn't see Clinton again before I left Arkansas. He was immediately incarcerated when the military militia apprehended him. The Colonel told me I should leave Arkansas immediately for the safety of my boys and myself. He advised me to go to Arizona where my parents had moved, and said Clinton would be given the choice between an extended jail term or serving in Viet Nam.

Clinton chose Viet Nam, and I chose not to move to Arizona to live with my parents. I had never lived alone, had my own apartment, or the freedom to make my own choices. I moved to New Mexico where, at least, I had a few friends. I sued for divorce, and Clinton wrote to me regularly, begging me to stop my divorce action. I didn't. Then one day he showed up on my doorstep, announcing he was on leave to "get his wife back." I couldn't believe he wanted to remarry me after the miserable five years we had shared. And I thought it terribly strange that he wanted to get married that same day. I knew something stunk.

Back in Viet Nam, without the benefit of marriage, Clinton finally wrote me a letter 'fessing up. A Colonel's daughter was pregnant, and she was naming Clinton as the father. Not wanting to marry the pregnant girl, he figured if he was already married to me, Colonel Fraser couldn't make him marry his daughter, Belinda.

Clinton would live to regret writing that particular letter.

12 - THE NOT-SO-GAY DIVORCEÉ

Life as a twenty-one-year-old divorcee with two small boys was not as easy as I had hoped it would be. Under normal conditions, it would have been hard for me to accept total responsibility for two small lives. I was still trying to learn how to take care of myself. But seizures started occurring more frequently, making it difficult to hold a job for very long.

Because I was never afforded the opportunity to be a child myself, I had little tolerance for normal child-like behavior in my sons. When either of them cried, I shook them and screamed at them to shut up. I loved both of them, but lacked healthy coping skills, so I resorted to what I knew: abuse under pressure.

I had been struggling for four months when a customer at the restaurant where I worked as a waitress asked if I would be willing to help his friend who was running for election. Thinking he meant stuffing envelopes, I agreed to help. One Sunday morning about 8:00, I was awakened by a knock on my door, and because I suspected it was the landlord trying to evict me again, I ignored the knock.

"Marilyn," the voice said, "this is Hal Mattner. Louie said you wanted to help in my campaign."

When I opened the door, I saw a dark skinned man about fifty, well-dressed and very professional looking. I asked him to sit down and then proceeded to make coffee for us as he began to explain what kind of help was needed.

"I'll send you to the salon to get the works, and then we'll go shopping for the best clothes. Then I'll show you the suites I've rented for the campaign. You'll have to look good for my visiting friends," he warned.

I was confused at first, but then I remembered something Mama had told me about a year before. Hal Mattner owned a chain of beauty colleges and Mama had her hair styled at one of them each week. She said every time she got a student who did her hair right, the girl would look sick for a couple of weeks and then "mysteriously disappear," leaving no trace of evidence as to her whereabouts. Mama said when she tried to question the other girls about the disappearances, one of them whispered she was better off not talking about it. Then the girl bent her nose to imply organized crime was involved. The girls who disappeared were always girls without family nearby to question the disappearances.

It was like a flash of supernatural knowledge came to me, and I knew, without anyone confirming it, Hal Mattner was a pimp working for the mob. The next thought was that I, too, had no family in El Paso to question my disappearance! I decided the best defense was a strong offense. I informed him I was not willing to be a prostitute for him or anyone else. He informed me his girls were not called prostitutes, and they fared far better than I was faring. The man knew every detail of my life! He had done his homework, knew I was struggling, knew I couldn't even pay my baby sitter, and he felt confident I would acquiesce because I had no choice.

Emboldened by something – or Someone – I'll never understand, I stood up to him and told him to get out of my apartment. He asked me if I knew what happened to girls who said "no" to Hal Mattner. His eyes narrowed and his facial muscles flexed as he tried to intimidate me. He should have never asked me that question. He never dreamt I knew the answer.

After I laid out for him what my parents and I knew about his operation (yes, I bluffed a little), he turned towards the door. With one hand on the doorknob, he told me I hadn't heard the last of him. I responded with a command to leave immediately, capping it off by calling him "Mr. Rat." I breathed a sigh of relief as I heard his Cadillac peel rubber on the street.

That night I went to work only to find out that I had been terminated. No one knew why, or even who, but they knew I no longer worked there. As I walked the streets for the next two weeks, applying for job after job, only to be told the position had already been filled, I knew who was responsible for my inability to find work: Mr. Politician Rat. I knew the positions weren't filled: they had "help wanted" signs in the window. As soon as each prospective employer saw my name, he nervously told me the job was taken. But the signs stayed in the windows.

With no options left, I packed everything I owned in a '56 Chevy with no ball bearings in the wheels, and headed for Arizona to live with my parents. I wasn't sure the wobbly car would make it, but I had no choice. It was one of the lowest points of my life.

~~~

Phoenix was hot, and living with my parents again was unbearable. Still unable to disconnect from Mama except through rebellion, we fought most of the time. It angered me when I saw her treating my sons the same way she had treated me as a child. She didn't beat on them, but they could never do anything right, and she used that same overbearing, condescending tone with them I knew all too well.

I found a job at a credit collection agency, but I didn't last long because I felt sorry for the people who owed the money and couldn't pay. I was fired so they could hire someone who could stay detached: someone who didn't get so emotionally involved with the deadbeats.

The next job was in the one-girl office of a vending

machine business, and my boss insisted I wear three-inch heels and black nylons to work. He then positioned my desk so my legs would always be visible to him as he sat at his desk. He said the sexual energy helped him sell more aggressively. I felt violated every day, but trapped. As aggressive as I could be at times, I could not, in this situation, muster up enough confidence to tell this jerk I would not be used like this. I felt paralyzed and victimized.

Life at home wasn't any better. It was painfully obvious no one there was happy. My sons and I felt like we were walking on eggshells, or in a minefield. The addition of constant stress, added to my lack of coping skills, was like pouring lighter fluid on burning logs. I was an out-of-control mother living as an out-of-control daughter in a home where no one was happy. I began to act out my anger by throwing things at the walls.

I still didn't understand why Daddy had left the last church so quickly, but I did notice he was hardly ever home. Those rare times when he was home were spent locked in the den watching wrestling matches and reruns of "Gunsmoke." One thing for sure, he was not a happy man when he was home. I noticed he had bought several new suits and he began dressing flashier: younger. And he traded in his car for a sporty red Mustang. And then he showed up one day driving a pickup with a nice camper installed. He said it was for the fishing trips prescribed by the doctor to relieve stress. But he wouldn't take his grandsons fishing in it.

Mother, unhappy herself, complained about the lack of affection from Daddy. In the role reversal she had initiated, she used me as her confidante, sharing intimate details about their past sex life, just as one would talk to a mother. I felt extremely uncomfortable with this arrangement, but helpless to do anything about it. It felt unnatural: almost like incest.

One day Daddy was persuaded to take Mark with him in his new camper, and he told Mark he could have anything he wanted at the store. Mark was thrilled to have some badly needed male attention from his Grandpa; but when he came home seven hours later, Mark whispered to me that they had gone to see a nice lady who lived up in the mountains. He said Grandpa had made him sit in the cold truck for a long time before he let him come into the lady's house, and then they gave him games to keep him busy while they went into the other room. It was on the way home that Daddy stopped off at a convenience market and let Mark choose any candy he wanted; but he told him not to tell anyone where they had gone. I didn't say anything to Mama about it. I didn't want to hear them fighting.

Five days before Christmas I received my ticket out of my parents' home. I received a Christmas card from Les Moiré, the boy who had been away at military school when I married Clinton: the one I was "going steady" with. In the five years since I had given him back his class ring, he had not married. He had just been discharged from the Air Force and was attending New Mexico State University, majoring in Engineering. He wanted to know if he could come to Phoenix to visit me over the holidays! Could he!

He took me out in the Arizona desert, and as we stood all alone, gazing at the beauty of the stars, Les told me he had always loved me. He said he guessed he would love me until the day he died. I knew, the way only a desperate female knows, that Les Moiré was my ticket out of my parents' home.

~~~

Les and I were married in Juarez, Mexico, and I moved to New Mexico to live with him. Shortly after our marriage, we received a notice that Clinton and his mother were suing me for custody of Mark and John. Since Les was a college student, we had no money for a lawyer. Daddy suggested that I defend myself, even offering to help me prepare the case. Then all alone, I stood in the courtroom defending myself against the Furrows. Their lawyer argued that as an epileptic, I was "unfit" to give Mark and John proper care. Clinton, he argued, was not an epileptic, but a happily married man in a "stable" marriage, and gainfully employed with the State Department. Clinton lied on the stand, swearing that I had married him without telling him of my epilepsy: I had defrauded him. His lawyer pointed out that my husband was not even employed, and since I was the one working, who would care for the boys. He didn't mention that Les was going to school on the GI Bill, but chose, rather, to make it sound like we were destitute.

Then it was my turn to call witnesses. Daddy was my first witness, and then Clinton was my second witness. After all those years, Mama's obsession with paper collecting paid off. When I stuck Clinton's letter in front of his face (which Mama had saved) and asked him if he had written it, he said he had. When I asked him to read out loud the part where he had written how he had impregnated Belinda and was being forced to marry a girl he didn't even like, his face lost color rapidly. The more he read, the paler he became.

When I pulled out letter after letter (which Mama had saved), making him read out loud all the obscenities and threats he had written to me and to my parents, the judge got a good idea of how "stable" Clinton was.

When I asked Clinton to explain how he received the huge scar on the back of his hand, he stumbled, stuttered, and nervously looked at his mother. In the end, though, he had to admit he had received the injury by putting his fist through the door one night when I slammed the door to protect my son and myself from his violence.

When the judge handed down his decision, he told me he had never seen anyone better prepared in his courtroom. He said my defense was as professional as any lawyer who had ever stood before him. Daddy glowed as the judge complimented me. I had finally done something to make him proud of me.

The Furrows sneaked out of the courtroom without speaking to anyone. We all knew it was Mrs. Furrow, not Clinton, who wanted Mark and John. I took great pleasure in defeating her once again. It was a day I'll never forget: an almost perfect day for me. Janine was not in the courtroom. She had quit speaking to me the year before. She expected me to sing at her wedding, and didn't believe I could not afford to fly my boys and myself there. She didn't yet know how it was to be the poor mother of two small children, paying the baby sitter with a vacuum cleaner or a toaster because there was no money. But she would live to know that reality.

The next three years were peaceful for my sons and me. Les was basically passive, so we never had any arguments. He went to school, I worked, and he went along with any decisions I made. We moved to Iowa where he worked as a mechanical engineer for a tractor company, and on the weekends we traveled to Shabbona to see my Grandma. She loved being called "Grandma," and she gave my sons the grandmotherly love they couldn't receive from my mother.

My cousin Billy, who was two years older than I, drove his motorcycle to Iowa and stayed with Les and me for several weeks. Billy always was my favorite cousin, and when he and his sister lived in New Mexico during the fifties, it was Billy with whom I got into trouble most of the time. He liked living on the edge as much as I did, possibly because his father had a drinking problem and his mother abandoned him at a young age. During my twelfth and thirteenth years of life when I was feeling like the family freak, it was Billy who made me laugh. He and I both loved to take a dare, and as a result, we were usually in the doghouse.

One night as we were snowed in by the latest Iowa storm, we began to talk about the past. Les and the boys were asleep, and Billy and I were playing cards. I began to tell him how unhappy my father looked, and when I blamed Mama for his unhappiness, Billy startled me with his response.

"If your Mama is responsible for his unhappiness, then he must've been unhappy with her for a long time," he said.

When I asked him to expound on that statement, he started backtracking as he shifted his cards around. Something in the way he had said "long time" led me to believe he knew something I didn't know. Finally, after he saw I wasn't going to give up, he asked me if I remembered Rheba Roberts, the sexy redhead in New Mexico. Of course I remembered her! She was the one everyone accused of being a smoker! She was the one Patty and I had spied on! She was the reason I got such a whipping from Daddy when I reported the results of our spying! She was the one Mama never spoke to!

"Do you remember when Daddy wanted to leave New Mexico so he could get married again in Illinois?" Billy asked without looking at me. "Remember my sister Pat and I wanted to stay in New Mexico, but we didn't have anyone to live with because your mama's room was all filled with newspapers?"

"Yes," I answered impatiently, "what's that got to do with Rheba?"

"Well, Uncle Cal arranged for us to live with her until Pat married Ronnie, and one day I skipped school. Rheba worked, so she shouldn't have been home, but she was." Billy's voice had an edge on it and I knew he was going to draw out the story in typical Morston fashion, milking every last detail for enhancement. I lit a cigarette and decided not to play his game. He'd have to get to the point eventually.

"Well," he said with a mischievous half-smile, "want to know who else was there?" He was dying for me to bite, so I didn't.

"No, Billy, I think I don't want to know the rest of the story."

"Uncle Cal was there in all his glory!" he announced. "I went through the back door of Rheba's house and walked in on them."

"What were they doing, praying?" I asked facetiously.

"Praying! That's a funny one, Marilyn! Not unless it was some new religion I don't know about! They were lying in bed, naked as jaybirds, and each of them was smoking the 'cigarette after.'"

"You're making this up, Billy. You always were a storyteller."

"No, Marilyn, I swear to God it's the truth – swear to God!"

"What did Daddy say to you?" I challenged.

"He said, 'Now Billy, we don't have to tell anyone about this, do we?' and I said, 'No, Uncle Cal.' Then I turned and ran."

Suddenly everything made sense: all the fights Mama and Daddy had over Rheba, all of the time Daddy was gone from the house, and, most of all, the over-reaction Daddy had when I told him Patty and I had been spying on Rheba. He was afraid his nosey daughter would see them together, and he was afraid I would blab it to someone. His job was in jeopardy, and he was scared stiff that I would find out about his double life! Now I understood why he had distanced himself from me after that day. He was scared of me!

"You know what, Billy? That answers a lot of questions for me. Mama has always blamed my elopement with Clinton for them having to leave New Mexico. She's told me several times it was me who had disgraced her! It wasn't me – it was Daddy!"

"Don't you tell anyone what I told you, Marilyn – at least not until Uncle Cal is gone. I'll deny it if you tell anyone, i swear I will. But it's God's truth: you can call Pat and ask her if you don't believe me."

I promised Billy I wouldn't tell anyone, and I didn't. But all night long I remembered Daddy saying his brothers thought he was a "goody-two-shoes" because he had been so secretive. He joked about "if they only knew" like he was

88

proud of his duplicity. And I realized that Daddy had reacted to the pain Mama put him through with her seventeen-year-old musical protégé, Ron Schneider, by running to Rheba. Mama had emasculated him, using a teenager – not even a grown man! Rheba had given him back his masculinity, but at what cost?

Part of me was glad Daddy had found a woman to treat him like a man, and part of me was profoundly disappointed in his character flaw. I wondered if Mama ever knew, for sure, about Rheba, or did she suspect, the way an insecure wife does? And I realized there were probably many more secrets I didn't know about my father. I had just begun to see what a weak man Daddy was.

~~~

Living with Les allowed me to become more and more self-absorbed. Without confrontation or any call to accountability, I had free reign to do whatever I wanted, and be whomever I wanted. I needed someone to hold me accountable for my emotions, and I needed someone who cared enough to tell me I should get some professional help. Mark, my oldest son, was the compliant child and he never caused problems. John, my youngest – the son I never bonded with because of my long illness after his birth – was too much like me: stubborn.

John would lie about his behavior even when I caught him in the act. Each time he lied to me, something snapped inside and I reacted with rage. It was always his lies, not his disobedient behavior that triggered violence in me. When I was young and my mother lied to me, I had no power to express anger. But now that I was the adult, I wielded the power unmercifully, and John was my victim. The more he'd lie, the less control I'd have over my rage. I could see, in my moments of lucidity, the parallel between Mama's behavior and mine as a mother. I would have bet my life that I would never treat my own child the way I was treated, and yet, here

89

I was acting just like Mama. The self-loathing grew inside me and instead of taking responsibility for my own impulse control, I blamed Mama.

I hated that I was acting like Mama, especially when I knew how it felt to be abused. I hated that I was living with a man who, like my father, was passive and ineffective. I hated that, like my mother, I was overweight again. I didn't like anything about my life or myself when Les and I moved back to New Mexico in 1969. I was tired of being married, tired of being responsible for children, and bored to tears with my unexciting life. I was a full-fledged adrenaline junkie needing a crisis, or at least some thrills.

Daddy left his church in Phoenix abruptly, and he and Mama moved to a very small town in Texas, about 200 miles from where we lived. Thanksgiving, that year, was spent in their new home, with Janine and her husband, my family and myself. Daddy looked terrible: like a man tormented. He had gained more than fifty pounds, wasn't keeping up his appearance, and didn't seem to have any spark of life in him at all. After dinner everyone migrated into the living room to watch football, leaving me in the kitchen to do the dishes. It was the final straw for me. After twenty-five years of being designated as the family slave, I couldn't handle the anger. Just as I had seen my mother do so many times, I threw a violent tantrum that ended up in property destruction and "looks" from my father that told me he thought I was insane. Those looks would haunt me for many years. They would be the last I would ever see.

~~~

Mama called about once a month after Thanksgiving, trying to smooth my ruffled feathers; but she always managed to sneak in some personal advice:

"You need to lose weight, Marilyn. You're just ask- ing for trouble. Don't you know men leave wives for getting fat? Mark my words, honey, you'll lose a good man if you don't slim down."

Then came the tearful call. Mama told me Daddy had walked out on her and his church without even saying good-bye. He had gone back to Phoenix to be with Joy, the lady he had been having an affair with for more than three years. (This was all a surprise to me.) Joy was the lady who had given Daddy the camper; the "lady in the mountains" my son, Mark, had told me about the night he had to sit in the truck so long. She was the reason Daddy accepted the Phoenix pastorate, the reason he left abruptly – the members found out about the affair – and now she was the reason Daddy was abandoning his church without even resigning.

Mama told me she had been lying to the church members for three weeks, telling them he had been called to Illinois because his mother was dying. For three weeks Mama had kept all this to herself, thinking she could "fix" it and it would turn out all right! She said above all, things had to look right, even if they *weren't* right. She had to protect his reputation, she said. He was a man of God and no one could ever know about his nervous breakdown. It was more palatable for her to believe Daddy was sick – and therefore, not responsible – than to believe he was making a conscious decision to leave her. She lived in denial better than she lived in reality, and it didn't anger her at all that Daddy had left her with the responsibility of resigning for him! He needed her in his time of sickness.

I already knew Daddy was capable of infidelity; but I was shocked that he would treat his church with such disrespect. I had sufficient fear of God to also fear for the consequences of Daddy's irresponsibility. I had always believed that being a pastor was an honored position: a calling of God. How could Daddy just walk out of the ministry the way one walks out of a restaurant? I felt scared and disgraced. Leaving Mama was one thing; but leaving the ministry was something else. I feared God would not let Daddy's abandonment of his church go unpunished.

One month later my worst fears were confirmed.

~~~

It was 3:00 AM when I stumbled from my bed to answer the phone. Les and I had just moved to California three weeks before: not enough time to memorize my way around this new house in the dark. It was Mama, and she sounded calm as she told me Daddy was gone home. Thinking she meant Shabbona, I became annoyed at her for waking me out of a sound sleep with such trivia. Evidently I also annoyed her with my obtuseness and she responded with that slow, condescending voice I hated so much.

"Marilyn, he's gone home to be with Jesus."

"This is not funny and I don't appreciate your games at 3:00 in the morning," I asserted as I slammed the phone in its receiver. I had just found my way back to bed when the phone rang again. This time Mama was not as calm as she had been, and she told me Daddy had called her from Phoenix three weeks ago, crying, mumbling he had no place to go. She had told him to come home to her and his church. She said his heart had been broken and it was "that woman" in Phoenix that had broken it.

Evidently, Joy had been able to live with an affair; but when Daddy left his wife and his church for her, it scared her so badly she ran out and married an ex-boyfriend for safety. Mama said Joy was a backslidden Christian who realized God would punish her big-time for causing a pastor to leave his ministry. It had been Joy and her mother who had traveled to El Paso as part of the "search committee" for a new pastor, and it was Daddy they had decided on. Now, four years later, Joy had come to her senses a little too late.

Daddy had called Mama from a bar in Phoenix, she said, and he had told her he ordered a beer and then just sat and stared at it for more than an hour, never drinking any of it. Then a troubled young woman had sat on the barstool next to him and he had just started witnessing to her about Christ and how to be saved. He told Mama he knew he'd never be able to preach again, and he knew he couldn't live without preaching. He was lost between the world of the saved and unsaved, not fitting in with either group. He wanted to die. He never suspected Joy would hurt him so badly, and the pain of what she had done to him – and what he had done to God – was too much to bear. Of course, he'd never commit suicide. He was afraid of how God would feel about suicide. Mama said he told her even she had never hurt him as bad as Joy did.

Mama was anxious to rescue Daddy once again from disgrace, and she told him to come home and they would pretend this never happened. And he did. He resigned his church and they moved to a small cheap apartment in El Paso. Mama was still working, so they lived on her money for the three weeks he was alive. Daddy had no idea of how to go about getting a job at the age of forty-six. All he had ever done was pastor, and his will to live was gone. He sat and watched daytime television while Mama worked.

"Then last night, right in the middle of sex," Mama was now reporting, "he just died: just fell on me like dead weight." She had called the ambulance and they had carried Daddy to the hospital without turning on their lights or siren. Mama said she kept begging them to turn on the siren, but they had said Daddy was already dead and there was no hurry. Daddy had wanted to die, and he had.

~~~

Patty accompanied Les and the boys and me on our journey from California to El Paso for Daddy's funeral. It was scheduled for the day after Thanksgiving, so all the guests would have a long weekend and could make it in time for the ceremony. Janine and her husband came from Phoenix, and hundreds of people from New Mexico came to bury their ex-pastor.

I never cried. All the way from California to El Paso, I cracked jokes and kept myself well insulated from grief. I had not been able to cry since I was very young: a decision I had made after one of Mama's especially violent beatings. Very early I had learned how to shut off physical pain: how to disconnect myself from my body completely. It always angered Mama more when she whipped me and I refused to cry. It was my version of control. I had become so adept at not feeling pain that now I could not feel pain even when it was appropriate. What had begun as a voluntary decision was now in control of me.

In my state of emotional paralysis, I knew I could sing without breaking down. I had sung at dozens of funerals, and this one was no different – at least, not to me. But Mama wouldn't hear of it. She wanted the funeral to run smoothly, and she was sure I'd do something to bring disgrace to the memory of my father. Even in her loss, Mama was adroitly in control, polishing the image of Reverend Calvin Levi Morston.

I couldn't believe how many people attended Daddy's funeral. I kept wondering where all these people were coming from? I wished they would all go home and leave him alone. Mama kept insisting that I take "one last look" at Daddy before it was too late. I didn't want to remember Daddy as some lifeless being. I wanted to remember him telling jokes, robustly singing hymns, playing softball at church picnics, and throwing church kids up in the air after Sunday School. But Mama wouldn't let it be.

At the end of the funeral, Mama created a scene in front of everyone, shaming me for not looking at my own father. Finally, embarrassed by Mama's accusations, I acquiesced, walking to the casket and looking at the body inside. In that split second, my eyes saw only a green face that looked nothing like the father I loved.

The next thing I saw was hundreds of people standing around me as I lay on the floor screaming uncontrollably: no tears, just screaming. Janine was mortified at my "inappropriate behavior," and Mama regretted insisting that I look.

Even at the cemetery when the military trumpets played "taps" and they lowered Daddy into the ground, I never cried. The anger I felt fortified me through all of the ceremonies and all of the business we had to take care of afterwards. I was angry with Mama, but mostly, I was angry with God who could pull such a cruel joke on me: taking Daddy and leaving Mama behind with me. Now any chance I might have had to win his love was gone forever.

~~~

The crowds pushed and pulled at my body and I couldn't see over the taller heads in the crowd. Standing on my tiptoes, I saw Daddy up ahead and screamed for him to turn around; but Daddy did not hear me. My heard pounded harder as I tried to push my way through the crowed, but no one would step aside to let me through. No one would let me through!

"Daddy!" I screamed, "it's me, Marilyn! Over here, Daddy! In back of you, Daddy! Can't you hear me? Daddy! Look at me! It's me, Daddy!"

My heart sank as I realized Daddy would never hear me: too many other people were in the way. It was the same old story: he noticed everyone but me. I tried to cry, but no tears would come to the forgotten child this night. Like lead, the weight of knowledge pinned me down. Daddy would never notice me. He noticed every one *but* me.

It was that haunting dream again, and it wouldn't go away. I got out of bed and walked to the bathroom, hoping it would help me shake the feelings of the nightmare. But back in bed, the dream continued:

I was driving down a highway and saw it again: the huge billboard with Daddy's face on it, bigger than life. Why was his face on the billboard? Why couldn't I reach up high enough to touch his face? Why wouldn't he look at me? My heart ached to touch his face, feel his arms around me; but he was only a billboard. Billboards can't love their daughters.

"Billboards are just for show, Marilyn," Daddy's eyes were saying. "Billboards are there to sell fantasy; they're fake. Billboards can't feel, and they don't care what you feel. They're just like your life, Marilyn: *just for show*."

"Sit up high on that dangerous pedestal, Daddy, and JUST LOOK GOOD, no matter how you feel," I said in my mind.

"We're all on that pedestal, aren't we, Daddy?"

"We're all falling, aren't we, Daddy?"

14 - NEW BIRTH, NEW BEGINNING

Les and I were back in New Mexico and he had just graduated from New Mexico State University. His schooling had taken longer because of the work program he was on: going to school six months, moving to get practical experience as an engineer, then moving back to New Mexico. I liked moving around. It agreed with my gypsy nature. One thing was missing from my life, though: a daughter. When my tubes were tied at age twenty, I just gave up on ever having a daughter. But someone suggested that Les and I look into adoption, and we did. For nine months we filled out papers, sat through interviews, and waited to hear what our references said about us. Naturally, I made sure we were involved in a church. Giving a minister as a reference would look good, I thought. Our lives were interrupted constantly as the New Mexico State Welfare Department investigated every corner of our existence.

Nine months after we started the process, we had our daughter. She was the most beautiful girl I had ever seen: turned up nose, rosebud mouth, and wide blue eyes that would later turn brown to match her light brown hair. She was born in El Paso, like the boys, and she was half Cherokee Indian just as the boys were. Having Clarissa was like a dream come true and I resolved to be the best mother in the world.

I quit smoking so Clarissa wouldn't be harmed by secondary smoke, quit my job so I could be a full-time mother, and started learning how to be domestic. I wanted her to have the kind of mothering I had never experienced. I made semi-peace with God – sort of a "cold war truce" – since He had blessed me with a daughter; but my heart was still bruised with the belief that He valued everyone but me. I

97

lived for Clarissa, holding her every minute I could. I watched her sleep, learned to sew for her, and began to feel good about myself as a mother.

We were on our way to California where Les would start a new job, and we decided to spend Christmas in Las Vegas.. The boys were thrilled with all the lights and confusion, and Les, a lover of wine, was glad to be in an environment that didn't frown on drinking. Christmas Day was exciting for everyone. Les and I arranged for a porter to play Santa and deliver the gifts to the children, and then we ate a delicious Turkey dinner at one of the better restaurants. I had a new camera and I annoyed everyone with my constant picture taking. They told me I was just like my own mother.

It was the most expensive Christmas I had ever spent, and one I would never forget.

~~~

I cannot think of a more inappropriate place to receive the news. I'm standing in a loud, smoke-filled casino, obsessively feeding money into the one-armed bandits, hoping to leave Las Vegas and return to California as the riches twenty-six year old lady of 1970. I am laughing as I watch Little Richard swish past me in his overdone make-up and uni-sex ruffled tuxedo when I hear myself being paged over the p.a. system. Mama, from her phone in El Paso, has summoned the State Highway Patrol in Nevada to track me down and give me the bad news: *she* has lost her mother-in-law.

As I hold the phone in my hand, I am only half-aware of Mama's non-stop voice. I am feeling the impact of my own loss: my Grandma, my confidant, and, perhaps, even my angels. My mind travels back to a safe place of comfort and uncomplicated love: Grandma's house in the summer of '55.

That night as Grandma was tucking me into her

featherbed, she told me about the angels: how she prayed every night Jesus would send guardian angels to watch over me in New Mexico. She held me in her arms that night, looked at me through spectacles wet with tears, and told me how much Jesus loved me, even if I sometimes did naughty things. She asked me if I believed Jesus' angels were with me all of the time, even if I couldn't see them. And because Grandma was the one praying for them, I believed her. I knew Jesus would surely hear *her* prayers. She promised me that as long as she was alive, she would be praying for angels to protect me...

Now, standing in the noisy casino, I am once again aware of my surroundings. I hang up the phone, walk slowly through the casino, heading for the refuge of the bathrooms. I walk past dozens of old women parked in front of their slot machines, nickels in their coffee cans. I bump into the cleavaged blonde hanging on the drunken bald man, and I smell the odor of stale cigarette butts and warm beer. I see Little Richard with his red lips, his red acrylic nails banging on the piano as he screams, "Good golly, Miss Molly, sure love to ball." I look at the faces of the young prostitutes working the room, and I wonder if they have angels watching over them. I see blurred painted faces turning ugly with greed and then panic, as money is lost. I hear shrill female screams and shrieks as the dice are rolled to decide their fate. A stumbling three-piece-suit sways into my path and asks me how much I'd charge for a good time. I feel how much Grandma would hate this place, and my stomach begins to heave. I need to be alone. I need to escape the insanity of this brightly-lit asylum. I run to escape the inmates, and I find sanctuary in an empty stall just in time to puke into the toilet.

Alone in my stall, I am not alone. For the first time, I can feel the presence of Grandma's angels. Two of them stand guard at each corner of my stall. Liquid escapes from every orifice of my body. Unable to cry for all those years, my backed-up floodgates open, and it is hours before they close again. Oddly, not one person knocks at my stall in all that time. I know Grandma must be assisting the angels: she must be watching the years of pain dissolve down the drain. She must be holding me the only way she can, encouraging me to "let it all out." And I do.

~~~

Once we arrived in California we discovered that the company that had hired Les after receiving his application from New Mexico, had subsequently discovered he had a medical discharge from the Air Force. Actually, nothing was wrong with him: he faked a bad back to get out of the Service early. Now it had caught up with him. They couldn't hire someone who would present insurance problems. Here we were in California with no money and no job. It was my opportunity to come through, just as Mama had always done, and rescue my husband. I found a job as an employment counselor, which gave me access to all the available jobs in the area. In the meantime, I drove us to one of the churches and told them our story. They found a family willing to take all five of us in until we could afford our own place. The family was kind, but it was degrading to have to live in a stranger's home. To make matters worse, a robbery was committed while they were at church and they implied we had robbed them. We hadn't: we were out house hunting.

The stress of Grandma dying and then being destitute took its toll on me. My nerves were frazzled and my tolerance for John's lying was nil. It seemed like I was always out of control with him, and I hated who I was becoming. Les decided he didn't like being an engineer, after all, and decided to become a long-haul truck driver. I was left alone to handle all the stresses while he was gone for days at a time. My days were spent running to school – John had just kicked a teacher – or running to stores – John had been caught shoplifting again. Mark, more compliant, was quiet and made good grades in school, just as my sister

Janine had done. John was a carbon copy of his mother, and that's what made his behavior such a bitter pill to swallow. His acting out caused me to lose control, and my loss of control caused John to act out worse. It was a vicious cycle, and I knew it would only get worse.

One night, home alone, I saw a show on television about child abuse. I was surprised to find out there were so many other parents like me who were now learning to cope with frustration without beating on their kids. The woman said one of the problems was that these abusive parents were never allowed to be children when they were young, so they now had unrealistic expectations of their own children. They couldn't tolerate normal childish behavior. She said support groups were forming all around California to help these out-of-control parents, and I decided that night I was going to attend one of them.

The leader of the group I attended was an ex-prostitute and she seemed to take great delight in poking fun at me during the meeting. It was a twelve-step program, like Alcoholics Anonymous, and they talked about a "Higher Power," but never gave the power a name. When I had the audacity to name my higher power "Jesus," the leader swooped down on me like an eagle targets a scared rabbit. She told me I was a f---ing Pollyanna, and she asked what Jesus had done for me lately: why was I out of control if Jesus was such a big shot? I looked around the room as I was being ridiculed, and even in my out-of-fellowship state, I knew the ocean could never be my Higher Power. I decided to start a group of my own where people could call Him GOD.

I went back to my county and put an ad in the news-paper that read: "Can't cope with your kids? Call 555-2424." Then I sat at my typewriter and wrote letters to every church in my county, asking only for a room to meet in once a week. Out of 258 churches, only one responded. I was both angry and ashamed of the lack of concern church people had for others with *real* problems. It was as if church people didn't want to be identified with anything as repugnant as child abuse! They certainly weren't going to admit it might exist in their churches! I began to see church people like I saw Mama: caring only about appearances, not about reality.

The pastor of the one church that did respond was not only willing to open one of his rooms to me, but also volunteered to "sponsor" the group. He encouraged me to find other professionals to form a Board of Trustees, and also mental health professionals to sit in on the meeting each week.

For three weeks I sat in that room by myself, and then on the fourth week two people showed up for the meeting. For lack of a better format, I chose that of Alcoholics Anonymous, knowing the group would need to be structured if it was to be effective. Daddy had attended AA with several of his church members, and they did quit drinking, so I thought until I could find a better format, I'd use the twelve steps.

I told my story over and over for the next year, every Thursday night in the meetings, and one by one, each new member began to open up and admit her own shameful behavior. Each meeting had a mental health worker present to keep the meeting structured, and soon we needed another room for a second meeting. The community took notice of our success, and then the media began to invite me to tell my story to their viewers and readers. At the end of the first year I was endowed with celebrity status for which I had never been prepared; but I kept on my "happy face" and responded to every inquiry, filled every need, and lived up to every expectation. I was playing savior to anyone who needed me, rescuing everyone but myself.

By the end of my second year, there were thirteen chapters of my non-profit organization throughout California and Nevada. My workweek – for which I received no monetary compensation – was now 120 hours as I traveled to universities to "spread the gospel of rehabilitation." In 1971 I testified before the California Senate which resulted in stronger child abuse laws.

By the end of my third year, I was founder and executive director of my non-profit organization, with an impressive board of trustees. Doctors, lawyers, congressmen, health care professionals, and judges were singing the praises of this "Joan of Arc" who was giving her life to help others without regard for her own needs. I was the most talked-about lady in California, especially in my own county where social workers and judges were sending offenders to me in lieu of jail time for their offenses.

The premise was simple: if the parent can be rehabilitated it will save the county the cost of jail time and foster care for the children. One reporter told me that I, alone, had saved the county five million dollars in one year! This same reporter did a five-day spread on me, which showed up on the front pages of other newspapers.

I felt like I was doing what I had been born to do: to preach as my father had. Even though my message was different, I felt we both were rescuing the perishing, caring for the dying. Standing in front of a crowd of women hostile to child abusers, I felt the same kind of challenge my father must have felt as he stood before unbelievers. My job was to raise the consciousness of these status-conscious women, help them understand why child abuse occurs, and persuade them to financially support my mission. I looked into cold eyes as I explained that most of these parents had never been shown any alternative to child abuse: it was the way they were raised, themselves. I asked why we would condemn someone for not giving what he or she doesn't have. I explained that child abuse was cyclical, multi-generational, and unless it was stopped in this generation we would have another generation of child abusers.

My impassioned pleas, combined with my entertaining ability brought sufficient funds to keep the organization afloat.

And because I was no longer beating on John – I had learned alternative responses from the health pros – everyone believed I was emotionally healthy. But I was dying inside.

The pedestal I had allowed myself to be placed upon began to teeter, and my marriage was falling apart. Les was gone most of the time, driving his truck and drinking with his buddies. I had given away far more than I had to give for four years, and now I was emotionally bankrupt. My ego needs had driven me to the top, and once I arrived, no one was there for me to tell my troubles to. Everyone expected me to be strong, represent the organization with dignity, and continue my evangelism for child abuse prevention and cure. I WAS the organization. Without me, it would surely fall apart. I realized that this must be how Daddy felt before he died. After all, where does the spiritual leader go when he needs spiritual counsel?

I was rescuing, feeling victimized and becoming bitter: the same pattern I had noticed in Mama years before. I had stopped attending church because I was offended at their lack of "social concern," and now I didn't have time for reading the Bible or even praying. I was carrying this heavy burden all by myself. I wasn't mad at God, exactly. I just disliked and distrusted His people and didn't want to associate with them. They were just ostriches with their heads in the sand, unwilling to soil their appearances with anything as shameful as child abuse. My years as a pastor's daughter had taught me about church politics, and I didn't want any part of it.

Caught up in my "mission," I was extremely vulnerable to those whom I trusted, like the pastor who sponsored my first chapter. He drove me from one television studio in Los Angeles to another, as I shared my story with each newscaster and talk show host. He called me every morning to ask how I was doing, and he kept me believing in myself. I had lost sixty pounds, was not eating properly, and was getting very little sleep. I depended upon this pastor to "take care of me: rescue me." I was beginning to feel more and more helpless inside as I tried to do more and more to please the Executive Board.

One Saturday morning, after four years of nurturing, he began to use obscene language over the phone as he graphically told me all I needed was sex. His words paralyzed me in the same way I had been paralyzed in the airport so many years ago when I had followed that psychiatrist to his hotel room. As if hypnotized, I followed his instructions: I went to his office and watched him rape me on the carpet of his office. It was like it was happening to someone else. I never resisted, for it seemed to confirm what I already knew deep down inside. I wasn't as good as everyone was saying I was. Inside, I was still a bad girl who brought shame to everything I touched.

One week later I lay in a hospital bed with needles in my arms, crying because no one loved me. The doctors told me it was "mental exhaustion," but I knew it was a nervous breakdown. Outside, the public sang praises of this "sacrificial lamb," expressing their gratitude, and undying love for me. For two weeks I was fed intravenously as I cried non-stop. Humpty Dumpty had tried to be all things to all people, and now she was broken into a thousand pieces.

Before he released me, Dr. Monohan, the attending psychiatrist, advised me to leave the organization I had founded. He said I was "emotionally drained to the point of bankruptcy," and it would kill me to get back into my "Joan of Ark coat of armor." He advised me to find some "no-stress, fun employment" and try to find a will to live again. Then the same county that had gladly used me to save them millions on foster care and jail terms now informed me that they would not pay for my hospital bill. I felt profoundly alone, profoundly used, and profoundly unloved. It was perfect timing: used-up-victim meets perceptive persecutor. His name was Larry Jordan.

I met him at an audition for a little theater production. He was older, worldly, charming, and a great singer. He was an experienced persecutor and knew patience was the key to bagging his prey. He never made any advances toward me until after he talked me into going on the road with him as a singing duo act. He made all the arrangements, picked out my wardrobe, and then we piled Mark and Clarissa into my Volkswagen van and headed for Washington. John, it was decided, would stay with Les and ride with him in his truck. I knew I couldn't handle a disciplinary problem in hotels if I wanted to keep my gigs.

It didn't bother me much to leave Les. What I perceived to be unqualified love in the beginning of our marriage, I now saw as a refusal to get involved in a relationship. It was easier for him to isolate himself with a couple bottles of wine and fall asleep listening to John Denver songs. In his own way, Les had abandoned me just like my father did: with indifference and unavailability. I would have preferred to live with someone who battered me: at least there would have been involvement. I couldn't live with nothingness anymore.

What I didn't know about Larry Jordan before we left, I found out in Nevada, Washington, and every state in which we performed. He was a serious drug addict, an alcoholic, addicted to pornography, and more violent than any one I had ever known. What he did to me would take years to heal. What he did to my children will never be healed. I stayed on the road with him because he scared me with his Mafia stories, and also, I had no place to go. Les had moved out of the house and donated all our belongings to the thrift store. He had placed John with foster parents, telling them that I had abandoned him and would never want him back. Les didn't want the responsibility for John, and he was willing to pay someone to relieve him of it.

Unable to pray, but feeling the survival instinct within me growing, I began to read self-help books. I tricked Larry into thinking I was swallowing the powerful tranquilizer, Nebutol, he forced on me, and after he passed out I would lie on the floor and search for answers in my self-help books. Because Larry monitored my mail and my phone calls, and because he had sworn to kill my kids and me if I tried to bail out on him, I had to do some fancy footwork to plan my escape. All of my calls were made in public phone booths, but Larry still knew something was brewing. I had told him our next gig was in California, thinking I could at least find somewhere to hide in familiar surroundings.

That night as I lay sleeping in my separate hotel room, Larry opened my door with the key he had talked the clerk into giving him. As "Feelings" played loudly on my radio, I was raped, sodomized, and beaten senseless.

It felt familiar.

Safely back in California, I found a solo job as a piano bar singer, and soon I had an apartment for Mark, Clarissa and myself. It was the first time I had ever had my own place to live, and I loved it. I tried to locate Les, but he wouldn't be found. I wanted to know where John was, but Les was not about to give me the chance to ask him. He was afraid I would take John back, and then not be able to handle him. Then he'd "be stuck" with him again. He preferred to pay a foster mother to handle him. There wasn't much I could do since I had given Les legal custody of John in our divorce agreement.

Larry kept stalking me, calling with threats of bodily dismemberment at all hours of the night; but I filed each report with the police and swore out a peace bond against him. Then one day he burst through my door, and in front of my children, beat me into unconsciousness, banging my head on the rug-covered cement floor. Mark called an ambulance after Larry left, and then stayed with Clarissa while the drivers loaded me into the ambulance. Mark had become a surrogate parent to Clarissa at the young age of twelve. He had never been permitted to have a childhood of his own. It had been too easy to dump parental responsibilities on him because he was "so responsible."

Dr. Pugno was the resident physician on duty when they admitted me, and he chose to be my follow up doctor, too. He never left my side. He spoke with wisdom unlike any human being I had ever heard, and I wondered if he was one of those angels Grandma prayed for. He knew me by reputation – my child abuse crusading – and he listened with compassion as I spilled out the details of my wretched life. Then he looked me straight in the eye and told me I was bent on self-destruction. He said if I didn't get out of this dangerous relationship, he would personally have me committed to the state hospital. I remembered the frightening letters Patty's mother had written while she was committed, and I knew I did not want to be committed!

Dr. Pugno ran several tests on me that confirmed a hunch he had: he believed I had never had epilepsy. He told me my EEG was normal, as was my brain scan. Then he asked me if I had ever heard of Conversion Hysteria. I hadn't. He said it was a psychological disorder, and he gave me the example of the soldier who, on moral grounds, is opposed to killing. When placed on the front lines, the soldier's right arm will become paralyzed, making it impossible for him to shoot the gun (if he's right-handed.) His brain converts his hysteria into an actual physical handicap.

Then he asked me why I was living such a self-destructive life, and because he looked concerned, but not judgmental, I responded.

"I've never cared about the sex, Doctor. I just was afraid to sleep alone, afraid a seizure would kill me if there were no one there to control me. *I've always needed someone to control me*," I cried.

"Marilyn, you've just said a mouthful in that last sentence. You have serious emotional problems caused by the abuse you experienced as a child. You have done what you had to do to survive, and you're to be commended for surviving. The tools you used for survival were appropriate for survival, but they are no longer appropriate. You need help now to learn to live in a healthier way." Dr. Pugno moved in closer as he continued. "I believe you are not an epileptic, Marilyn. I think what you have is called Conversion Hysteria, and when you start taking personal responsibility for your life, and start living in a way that's consistent with your own moral values, your seizures will stop. There will no longer be any need for you to destroy yourself whether you're awake or asleep. There will no longer be any need to control the behavior of other people with your seizures, and there won't be so much anger to propel the seizures."

I was listening with great interest now that someone was, in essence, telling me I was not a freak. He was saying I could be different!

"You've tried to find yourself in everyone but you," he said. "Somewhere along the line, you've believed you were responsible for everyone's pain, and, therefore, the great fixer of their pain. You are destroying yourself with that lie. God never meant for you to be the savior of the world: He already did that, Himself. You are responsible only for you, Marilyn. You are responsible for your own nourishment, your own behavior, and your own feelings. You take care of others so you don't have to take care of yourself, and you end up feeling disposed of and used. Those who want to exploit you will tell you what you're doing is honorable, but it is not! God isn't honored, and neither are you."

I knew, without anyone telling me, that God had just spoken to me through this doctor, but I didn't know how to implement the changes I needed. I left the hospital promising Dr. Pugno I would think about what he had said, and went back to my job as a performer. Performing was easy for me: Mama had groomed me for it all of my life. I knew how to smile even when it hurt, how to please people at all costs, and above all, I knew the show must go on, no matter what. All of my energies went into creating another public self so I could continue to work in the entertainment world. I played the piano, sang, told jokes, and learned to hate what alcohol did to perfectly nice people.

I worked with an electronic drum, and when some one suggested I could make more money with a human drummer, I called the musician's union and asked them to send out prospective drummers. One of the drummers who came to my apartment to audition brought a friend who played guitar. His name was Alex, and he wasn't there to audition, but I felt drawn to him immediately. I saw in him all the pain I had felt, and I wanted to comfort him: to fix his pain. Now thirty-one, I saw this handsome twenty-one-year-old wounded soul and I was driven by the ghosts of my past to provide a healing balm for him. He touched something in the deepest part of me and I could not let him walk out of my life. I wondered if this was how Mama felt with her seventeen-year-old Ron Schneider.

One of the things that needed fixing in Alex was a relationship with drugs. I discovered it by accident when he disappeared for five days during Christmas of 1975. When he finally called me, he said he had just felt depressed and wanted to get loaded by himself for Christmas. This information did not send up red flags – or else I just chose not to see them. Instead, it only served to endear me to him even more. He needed someone to motivate him toward a healthier lifestyle, and I wanted to be the one who did it.

Larry was still terrorizing me with his threatening phone calls and I let Alex know about it. As the son of an alcoholic, Alex was well versed in the art of "crisis management," and he jumped into action to provide protection for this poor helpless woman. He didn't even need the white horse: he was my knight in cracked armor.

Alex's first night in my apartment was spent sitting upright in a chair, holding his loaded gun, waiting for Larry to show up in the wee hours of the morning. Larry never came, but the experience bonded Alex and me in an unhealthy alliance against my persecutor.

Two nights later, New Year's Eve of 1975, Alex and I played a gig with two other band members in a town forty-five miles away from home. At 3:00 New Year's morning, during the ride home, I laid my head in Alex's lap and he began to run his fingers gently through my hair. One of the other band members was driving, and we were in the back seat. Alex touched me with a gentleness I had known only twice before: Grandma and the medic, Reggie. My body went limp with relaxation, my mind floated pleasantly away from reality. I was instantaneously addicted to his touch. I gave myself to him that night without reserve. I was willing to pay any price to keep him.

Mark, now thirteen, did not want a stepfather. He wanted to be the only man in my life, and when he saw he wasn't going to get his wish, he became surly. Clarissa, now six, welcomed her new Daddy. She needed a Daddy. I still hadn't been able to locate Les, and didn't know where John was.

Life was not easy living with Alex. He, too, had serious problems with anger control, and it wasn't long before violence was erupting on a regular basis. I was more depressed than ever, and my dance with suicide picked up speed. Only the thought of leaving behind orphans stopped me.

I was driving home from the mall and because I had no current registration on my old car, an officer stopped me and asked for identification and registration. Naturally, he ran a check on me and discovered there was a warrant for my arrest. It was an old one, but still enough to cart me off to jail. After I had been released from the hospital and had no grocery money, I had written three bad checks at the grocery store that had totaled slightly more than $200: a felony in California. I had never made good on those checks.

At my arraignment several professionals who knew me from my child abuse crusading days came forward to offer testimonies of my character to the judge. He was not impressed. In fact, he said since I had been such a high profile person in the county, he would make an example of me. I got thirty days in jail.

~~~

Life in jail was different from anything I had ever known. There were no civilized rules to follow: the ever-changing rule of the toughest prisoner prevailed. Females sat around naked, passing gas, playing poker and talking about how they were going to get out and commit a bigger crime so they could go to a better facility. Toilets without stalls sat in the cell, giving prisoners no privacy at all. I spent the first week telling people I didn't belong there: I was a preacher's daughter. But after a week of not being permitted to sleep on my bed or eat my food, it began to sink in that I was where I was. I started smoking again.

Because I had a job, I was allowed out of jail every weekday morning at 7:30 to go to work. Alex picked me up and brought me back to jail at the end of the workday. The drug addicts in my cell demanded that I bring drugs to them since I was the only prisoner on work furlough. I didn't even know where to get drugs, and even if I had known, I would not have jeopardized my own "good behavior" time to do it. So a campaign ensued to keep me awake all night until I would bring in drugs. After my first sleepless week, all of my defenses were down and I cried out to God. I had met the bottom.

There was a Bible in the cell and I began to read it, but my mind was so scrambled from lack of sleep that I couldn't remember what I had read. At night as the prisoners would take turns hitting me to make sure I wasn't asleep, I tried to remember Scripture I had memorized as a child; but none would come to my mind. All I could remember was *"Yea, though I walk through the valley of the shadow of death, I will fear no evil: for Thou art with me,"* and I recited it over and over in my mind all through the night. Focusing on that scripture was the only way I had to keep from going over the edge. Then, slowly, a phrase at a time, old hymns began surfacing in my memory, and I began to sing to myself in my mind. The more I sang, the more I remembered. I was so grateful for the old hymns I had learned from childhood: they kept me focused on the character of God instead of my surroundings. It was like Grandma was with me in my bed, and we were singing all the old precious hymns together.

There was nowhere to run, no place to hide. I, like the prodigal son, had come to the end of myself, and now I had to trust God or die. I had three children who had no one but me, and I wanted to live; but, even more, I wanted to live *God's way*. My own way had not worked. Now I was ready to do whatever God required of me. I was ready to be whoever He wanted me to be. God would be in the driver's seat and I would be an obedient passenger. I was ready to face myself, and ready to face God. I had endured twenty-eight sleepless nights without losing my mind. It was the beginning of a new life for me.

I thought of her as a turtle. Each day she took her broom outside and swept the sidewalks around her property, knowing that within an hour they would all be dirty again. But, like a turtle, she plugged along making her corner of the world a little brighter and cleaner. Her consistency was a living testimony to me of living, on a daily basis, a God-honoring life no matter what mood she was in, no matter what others did. Her name was Liliane Wright and she was the first Christian that God brought into my life after I sold out to Him.

Liliane and her husband, Lew owned a triplex and they had been praying for Christian renters. When Alex and I answered their ad, Liliane knew immediately that God had sent us to them for a reason. When she found out I was a Christian, she was ecstatic. We moved into the apartment above them. She never asked about Alex's salvation, but it wasn't long until she found out there were some serious problems in this relationship. Violent outbursts, broken windows, and police officers coming to the apartment made it clear to her that all was not paradise upstairs.

I had an insatiable hunger for God's Word, and I spent most of my days devouring Scripture. Liliane knew how hungry I was, and as a mature Christian, she began to disciple me in the ways of the Lord. She loved me, laughed with me, cried with me, and became the mother I had needed all of my life. I called her my "God-mother" because I knew God had sent her to me. She had grown up in Africa as a Missionary's daughter, and had been raised by a father who loved her deeply. Lew, also a Missionary's son from Africa, had not had the advantage of loving, healthy parents, and it showed in his attitude. He knew the Scriptures, but he didn't exude God's Peace the way Liliane did. Over the months, Liliane shared how Lew had been hurt deeply by parents who expected him to continue the family tradition and be either a pastor or a missionary. Lew had wonderful gifts in business, but his parents constantly reminded him that he was being disobedient to "God's calling." He was an angry man.

Liliane helped me through some very difficult times as I tried to live God's way while I was living with a man who wanted nothing to do with God. Alex had, on several occasions, laughed with his brothers and sisters as they watched their Dad argue with the Christians who came to their door. They thought their father was brilliant when he asked each Christian where Lot got his wife, or other questions designed to ridicule those who dared to witness to him. Alex did not like my new way of living, and he not only ridiculed my faith, but also turned off the television if I was watching a Christian program. His anger mushroomed and he took it out on my children and me. Since we had not yet married, the apartment was leased in my name, giving me legal grounds on which to kick him out. Each time I did, he'd come back with new vengeance and we'd end up owing Lew and Liliane for broken windows.

In the middle of this mess, I began to have terrifying nightmares about demons. Most of them were similar to the same ones that had terrorized me as a child: female demons trying to destroy me and always being one breath away from success. But these dreams were fiercer and gripped me until I couldn't wake up. Alex would hear me screaming and try to wake me up, but it was like I was possessed by the nightmares. Liliane asked me if I really thought Satan was going to give me up without a fight, and she advised me to read the Psalms before I went to sleep. Then she reminded me that the name of Jesus had power to cast out demons.

About a week later I was in the middle of another nightmare. Several female demons had me cornered high in a tree and there was no place for me to go but down. Still dreaming, I pointed my finger at each demon, one by one, calling out their names, and commanding them, in the name of Jesus and through His shed blood, to be gone. As I pointed and spoke the name of Jesus, each demon disappeared, never to haunt my dreams again. It was one of those precious, private miracles God gives his young children to increase faith in His devotion. It was one of the blessings in my honeymoon with God that He would bring to my remembrance in dark days that would follow.

All of the years I had sat under my father's ministry, I never learned doctrine. I knew how to get saved, and I knew I was supposed to pray. But for all the Scripture I had memorized, I knew very little about God's ways. I had never read the Bible from cover to cover, so that's what I started doing. I had the help of Henrietta Mears' commentary (What The Bible Is All About), which helped me connect historical times, dates, and events. Prior to that, the Bible had just been a book of isolated scriptures to memorize.

As I went through the Old Testament I was shocked at what seemed to be the violent side of God. And the more I read, the hungrier I became. I saw God's personality become more and more complex, like a many-faceted diamond. Then as I reached the New Testament I saw the merciful side of God. I studied the Word with a fervor I had never known, and when I read what the New Testament said about divorce, I became confused and disturbed. What I was reading told me that because I was divorced and remarried – not once, but twice – I was causing Alex to commit adultery. God had already convicted me of living with Alex outside of marriage and a judge in Santa Barbara had married us shortly afterwards. But now this new information was a surprise to me! I needed God's blessing in my life, and I didn't want to do anything that would keep Him from blessing me. For weeks I agonized over what I should do. Did this mean God wanted me to go back to one of my previous husbands? After all, it's not like I hadn't been a Christian when I married both

117

of them – a disobedient child of God, but a child just the same. Would He really require that of me? Or did He mean for me to live alone for the rest of my life? I was making myself sick with worry when I decided to close the Bible, open it and see if God would give me a definite answer. The pages fell open to Isaiah 43, and certain passages just jumped out at me as living, breathing words:

"Fear not: for I have redeemed thee, I have called thee by thy name, thou art mine. When thou passest through the waters, I will be with thee; and through the rivers, they shall not overflow thee: when thou walkest through the fire, thou shalt not be burned; neither shall the flame kindle upon thee...Remember ye not the former thing, neither consider the things of old. Behold I will do a new thing; now it shall spring forth; shall ye not know it? I will even make a way in the wilderness and rivers in the desert."

I knew that God was giving me His personal promise for my life: He was telling me there would be wildernesses and deserts, but He would make the way and provide rivers for my refreshment. I knew He was telling me to forget the previous two marriages and all the mistakes I had made, and to move forward with Him. I knew He was calling me to make a commitment to marriage – and to Alex – and I knew it was to be a covenant: binding until death. I made the decision to trust God to work in my husband's heart as He saw fit.

I filled my mind with Christian music that lifted my spirits during the day, but my prayer times were filled with tears. God seemed to be saying that I had some amends to make, and the first was to my absent son, John. I felt God's urging to aggressively search for John, and on my knees each day, I begged God to lead the way and open the doors. The more I prayed, the stronger my desire became to have my son with me.

The second unction I felt from God was concerning

my sister, Janine. Mama had successfully pitted us against each other in order to ensure her own place in the family as "go-between." Neither Janine nor I trusted each other, and Mama liked it that way. At least, she knew we weren't "bad-mouthing" her to each other. She knew as long as she was our mediator, she would be indispensable.

I knew that Janine, now in her second marriage, was not walking with the Lord. I began to pray God would reach her as He had reached me. I asked Him to give Janine the same desire for a loving sister relationship and I began to write to her, making sure I communicated in loving, positive ways. Janine was distrustful of my motivation and she told me so; but I knew this was something God wanted, so I persevered. Even when Janine reacted with hateful insults, I remembered my promise to God: I would reflect Christ's love, no matter what.

~~~

Alex's old Ford Pinto was always in need of repairs, and Lew spent time teaching him how to keep it running. One day in 1977, Lew was helping Alex fix the car, and he challenged Alex.

"Alex, if I live my entire life for Christ, accepting His death as atonement for my sins, enjoying His peace and joy, but then die and find out there isn't really any Heaven waiting for me, what have I lost? While I was alive, I enjoyed all of God's blessings, so what did I lose?"

Alex didn't have a good answer for Lew, and in that moment all the years of antagonism for Christ faded as he accepted Christ as his personal Savior. It was a big step for the alcoholic's son who had been raised in the get-what-you-can-get-while-you-can-get-it ghettos of Detroit: the son who had fought to survive abuse, poverty, and shame. The man who prayed with Lew that day was the same boy who had been taught that "those Salvationists" were people to belittle; the child whose love for music was ridiculed; the child who had never known love or acceptance from anyone other than his teenaged partners in crime.

I was sure I heard Grandma's angels rejoicing that day as Alex decided to give God a chance to make something beautiful out of his sad, troubled life.

Lew lost his eyesight shortly after bringing Alex to the Lord: one minute he could see and the next he could not. He never regained it, yet even in his blindness, he crawled under Alex's Pinto and talked Alex through the necessary repairs. Alex marveled at the wealth of knowledge Lew possessed, as well as his ability to remember what he could not now see. As they spent time together, it became apparent that God had provided in Lew the godly father that Alex needed so desperately. He, too, had a "God-parent."

About a month after Lew lost his eyesight, Alex and I came home to find a strange car parked in front of our apartment. It was a well-kept used car that looked nice and ran even better. Lew and Liliane had spent the day car shopping for Alex, with Lew "seeing" through Liliane's eyes. The car was a gift, they said, and they asked only that Alex and I do the same for someone else some day. Alex had never known such unqualified kindness and he wept. He was learning about Christian love in a way that was concrete.

I, too, was learning that God truly cared for me. First, I was no longer having seizures, and no longer was taking Dilantin. It was just as Dr. Pugno had told me it would be. I was living in line with Scripture, and within my own moral value system, and the seizures were gone.

Also, one day – out of the blue – Les had a change of heart and divulged the location of John. Within hours Alex and I were on the road headed for Rialto, a three-hour drive away, where John was living with his foster mother. Alex had encouraged me to bring my son home even though he knew what possibilities could lie ahead. I had been openly honest about John, his behavior, and our relationship.

At first, John was afraid of me. He looked at me with distrustful eyes, remembering the lies his foster mother had told him. His mother never wanted him, she said, so he'd better shape up and fly right because he had no place else to go. With the help of The Holy Spirit, I was able to convince John that he was wanted by his mother, and he came home to be reunited with his older brother, Mark, and his younger sister, Clarissa. It was a mixed blessing for John.

Mark had felt like the "favorite son" for a few years, and he resented John getting all the attention. He was already angry about having Alex in the house – he wanted to be the man of the house – and now John's presence threatened his position as "only son." He took out his feelings on both his younger siblings in ways that would haunt both of them for many years to come. John, because he feared he might be sent away again, never told me about the abuse. It was better than not belonging.

Life with John back at home, and an inexperienced step-father for my children gave me daily opportunities to learn that even though God had forgiven my sins, there was still a crop that would be harvested from the seeds I had sewn for so many years. The seeds had been sown in ignorance and pain, but they would grow into plants just as surely as seeds sown any other way. God would have to give me sufficient grace to watch each species in the painful crop come to fruition.

17 - A NEW FRIEND SUCH A TIME

When I came to the Lord, I loved Him with all my heart; but I neither liked nor trusted His other children. Years of manipulation, abuse and hypocrisy had left me distrustful of "church people," and I had no desire to seek out their company. I was satisfied to stay at home with my Bible and have my Heavenly Father all to myself. I knew God wouldn't hurt me the way church people had hurt me. He wouldn't tell me everything I did was inappropriate for a preacher's daughter. I hoped God would stay with me in the refuge of my bedroom and allow me to hide with Him from the rest of the world. But it was not His plan.

Alex worked part time as a guitar teacher and one October day in 1977 he handed me the phone number of one of his students. He said he thought the mother of this student was a Christian. Her name was Anne. I waited two days before I called her, primarily because I suspected she would be like all of the other church people I had known. But when I heard her voice I knew she was not like the others. I asked her right off if she was a born-again Christian, and she cautiously answered that she was. A stranger had never called her and asked such a personal question in such an in-your-face way, she told me later.

We talked on that first day as if we had known each other all our lives. She was six months older than I, had four children, and lived only five minutes from me. We certainly had a lot in common! She, like I, had learned that church people could hurt each other, and she reasoned the pain was worse because our expectations of Christians were higher than those we had for non-Christians. We had both been raised in the church, and we had both walked away from it during our twenties. At thirty, we had both hit our bottom, recognized that we had made a mess of our lives, and had sold out completely to Him. We shared a hunger to know God more intimately and to live for Him, even in the midst of the consequences that we knew would come as a result of our years of disobedience.

Like me, Anne had known Jesus at an early age. The daughter of an alcoholic, she spent many of her young days on the bathroom floor begging God to change her father. Unknowingly, she had married a man who was in the first stages of alcoholism: the fun stage. As the marriage had progressed she had chosen to walk with him in the ways of the world. Like me, when she returned to her Heavenly Father, it was out of great personal pain. We were both deeply in love with Jesus, so He just naturally dominated our conversation. For over three hours, we talked of the unconditional love of Jesus and His amazing mercy. Anne appreciated my bubbly effervescence and I appreciated the unconditional acceptance I felt from her. It was a Jonathan-David friendship: each completed the other.

Three days after that phone call, Anne and I met face to face. She was one of the most beautiful women I had ever seen: dark hair, dark eyes that seemed to look deep into my soul, and a kind face that reminded me of my teacher, Margaret Trouissant. Her attitude was gentle like Grandma's. Known for my use of shock, I knew I would never be able to shock her out of loving me and accepting me just as I was. Anne was the sister I had always wanted, and I knew God had sent her to me. He knew what I didn't know: Liliane would be leaving California and I would need a Christian friend to help me on my journey. He gave me a godsister because He was moving my godmother away from me. He was, once again, proving Himself faithful to me.

~~~

Unable to work because of his blindness, Lew decided he and Liliane should move out of California. The cost of living was just too high for retired people. So they sold their triplex and moved to Oregon where life was less complicated and costs were down. In the months preceding their move, I had seen a noticeable change in Lew's attitude. It was as if losing his physical eyesight had increased his spiritual sight, making him peaceful and wiser. I hated to see them leave, but Alex and I promised to visit them as often as we could.

We accepted Anne's invitation to visit the church she had begun to attend, and we fit in right away, thanks to our musical talents. It wasn't long before Alex was directing the orchestra and I was playing piano and singing for the Lord again. All seemed to be going well, but at home we still had problems.

While salvation had changed Alex's heart, his years of abuse in the home of his alcoholic father had left their mark. His sensitive nature left him susceptible to rejection and pain, and anger was the only defense he knew. No one in his family had ever communicated anything but disapproval and ridicule, and Alex couldn't give to me what he, himself, had never received. And, while I truly loved the Lord and was trying to live in a way that would be pleasing to Him, I, too, had built up years of the kind of anger that only a victim would understand. Our fights at home made me feel shabby as we sat in church looking like the perfect couple. I felt a large chasm between what the Bible promised – abundant life – and what my life was in reality.

Anne was involved in a twelve-step program de- signed for codependents: people who shared alcohol dependency with a parent or a mate. Both of us avid readers, we began to swap books dealing with several subjects: doctrine, alcoholism, childhood abuse, wife battering, and codependency. I began to see a clear pattern in my life and I traced it back to both of my parents.

Even though my mother had never been a drinker, she displayed all the symptoms of the alcoholic because she had shared them with her alcoholic father. I began to question Mama about her parents and grandparents, and I saw the thread of alcoholism running from generation to generation. I also saw the threads of violence, sexual abuse, and suicide. I began to understand why appearances were so important to Mama: it was the only way to hide the shame that had been inflicted on each preceding generation.

Then I made a trip to Texas and Illinois to interview several of my father's relatives. I had huge memory gaps that spanned about five or six years of my childhood and I needed answers from those who knew me during that time. Also, I wanted to find out who my father was. If anyone could tell me who Daddy was, his relatives could. And they did. I began to understand why Daddy was so passive: he was like his gentle mother, not his abusive father. Grandma had been responsible for raising the girls, and Grandpa raised the boys. It was the way it was done in those days. He disciplined his sons with verbal and physical abuse, and he battered my Grandma. No wonder she knew I was being abused! No wonder she was so committed to praying for guardian angels for me!

Grandma dressed all of her six children and took them to church each Sunday where she taught her Sunday School class. But she was never able to stay for the worship service because Grandpa demanded lunch be on the table at precisely 11:30. She endured his abuse, his profanity, and pure meanness because she had nowhere to go. When Daddy, her youngest, came along, she spoiled him rotten. He learned to stay out of his father's way and as a result, he didn't get the beatings his older brothers got. He was always known as the good boy who never gave any one any trouble. He avoided confrontation like the plague and desired only to live peaceably with all men – and women. He was his mother's pride and joy, and she had given him the middle name of "Levi" after a visiting evangelist by the same name held a revival at her church. She always knew Daddy would be a preacher like "Rev. Levi."

I understood that because Daddy's mother had been responsible for raising the girls, it was logical that he would assume that was my mother's responsibility to raise Janine and me. And I understood that his passive nature allowed him to let Mama take over both the house and his ministry. I even understood why he didn't intervene in Mama's abuse of me. What I didn't understand was why he loved Janine more than he loved me. He held her all the time, but hugged me only one time that I could remember: when I was pregnant with John. I thought Janine could give me some insight into that question; but when I, in a state of depression, put all my feelings and questions on tape and sent them to her, she over-reacted. She was angry as she asked me why I couldn't forget the past and get on with living. Her reaction was so out of proportion to my request it made me suspicious. I had always been jealous of her special relationship with Daddy: it was like they shared secrets to which no one else was ever privy. I decided to call her again and press her for some answers, especially after a phone call from Mama that made me doubt my sanity.

~~~

Calling Mama long distance was something I tried to do as infrequently as possible. Mama didn't need much oxygen, and it was hard to get a word in edgewise. Always, Mama had interrupted with "Oh, before I forget..," and always, she had looked elsewhere while I talked to her. It made me feel she was not interested in what I was saying, so as the years passed I began to tell her less and less about my life. But when I was paying for a long distance call, it angered me that she never asked how I was, how the kids were, or show any interest in my life, except to ask if I had lost any weight. As she got older, she did as many senior citizens do: she told me stories about people I had never met, which would make her think of another story, and so it would go ad infinitum. The message was clear: she was interested in everyone's life *except mine*.

126

It was during one of these calls that she began to tell me about this poor little girl that moved in next door to her. She said she suspected her stepfather was beating the child. I asked her why she felt such pity for this little girl, but had never felt any for me. She said, "Why should I feel pity for you? You never got beat!" I heard Mama talking, but clouded by confusion, I heard her speaking through a distant tunnel. Then her words exploded in my mind. I instantly wanted to hit her, to hurt her the way she had hurt me. How dare she deny what she had done to me! My mouth struggled to form words: words that would decimate her. Absorbing the shock, I willed myself to breathe slower as alien feelings swept through me. Everything – memories, beliefs, assurances – seemed instantly out of focus. Still she kept talking. "Just tell me one time I ever hit you, Marilyn. Just one time!" I heard her challenge, but through the insanity that had seized me, she sounded unintelligible, remote. I thought one of us was totally insane, and I was beginning to think it might be me. Or maybe what she did was so abhorrent to her she had completely blocked it from her mind. Or maybe I was crazy and had imagined all of the abuse. After tormenting myself with a roller coaster of self-doubts for three days, I called Janine in Phoenix.

"Oh, Marilyn, why can't you quit living in the past?" she asked in an impatient and condescending tone. "The past is dead only if you're enjoying the present," she preached. "Why do you keep allowing mother to victimize you over and over? I'd think you would have more respect for yourself. Just accept the fact that mother is sick, and get on with your life, if you have one."

Feeling I had little to lose by pressing her, I insisted she tell me if she remembered Mama beating me all those years. I told her Mama denied it and I wanted to hear from her whether the abuse was "all in my head." By this time I was in tears, and Janine must have felt a spark of pity for me.

"No question about it, Marilyn. You got screwed,"

she confirmed. "Mother has lived in denial for so long she wouldn't know reality if it bit her; but it's you who gives her permission to keep you torn up now. It took me seven years of therapy before I could have a funeral for her: a real live funeral! And as far as I'm concerned, she's dead. I wish I were rich so I could just send her money every month and not have to talk to her. I've never understood why you keep trying to get her approval. I don't need her approval at all."

"No," I countered, "you never did need her approval: you had Daddy's approval."

"Approval?" she screamed, "don't you mean suffocation? Listen, Marilyn, I'll admit you got abused in ways I didn't. But you weren't the only one who lived with abuse." Then she added (for shock value), "Because of Daddy, I could have been an excellent prostitute! I already knew how to sublimate sexual desires – to shut off all feeling – and I could have become one very rich hooker!"

Janine went on to tell me why she had sucked her fingers and slept with Daddy until she was thirteen: Daddy made a "wife" out of her, telling her all his problems, secrets, thoughts, and feelings. She added, very quickly, that of course, he had never touched her "inappropriately." But she said she could feel Daddy – all of him – as he lay behind her, and while she felt sexual urges – and could feel that Daddy did, too – she knew she couldn't do anything about them. She said Daddy made her life miserable because he wouldn't let go of her: she was his emotional hostage, even after she married. She said he continued to show up unannounced at her home expecting her to function as his emotional pit stop. She said if Daddy had a real wife, he wouldn't have needed to make one out of her. She hated both of her parents, and said she would have traded places with me any day of the week.

After our conversation, I realized Janine's damage had been even more insidious than mine, and if I had been able to pray, I would have thanked God Daddy hadn't

"loved" me like he had loved her. Our conversation had answered many of the questions that had plagued me for years, but still I was gripped by depression so severe that I despaired of life and played with the idea of ending mine on a daily basis. There was no clear-cut cause that I could see – no reason or rhyme to the despair. I knew if I was going to live very long, someone had to help me get past the pit. I knew how both of my parents felt about psychology garble: "If you're a Christian, you don't need to get advice from anyone but Jesus." But their biases could not deter me from what I knew I needed. It was survival time, and I needed professional help to survive.

18 - SIFTING THROUGH THE RUINS

It was a hot, humid morning in early July. I was sitting in the waiting area of the Robert Mueller Municipal Airport in Austin, waiting somewhat nervously to board a flight back to California with a stop over in El Paso where my mother would be waiting to see me.

Over the last two years I had been attending therapy sessions with a Scripture-based therapist, searching for truth about my own beliefs about who God was. I had spent hours each week writing inventories, trying to find out how I felt at my deepest level about various subjects. I had started a page entitled, "ALL MEN ARE..." and had discovered, to my amazement, I had a very low opinion of men. Another, entitled "ALL MEN SHOULD BE..." showed me the chasm that existed between my idealized perception of men and my real opinion. Another page, "GOD IS..." revealed a warped perception that was very much like how I saw my parents.

One very difficult inventory entitled "MY MALE RELATIONSHIPS..." had me listing every male in my life – from my present all the way back to Daddy – and writing down what I had given and received from each one. A definite pattern emerged that left me in shock, but wiser: every single male in my life had used me, and I had allowed it. Some used me to tear away from their dominating mothers, some for sexual reasons, some for their own ego gratification, some for what they perceived as courage, some to fill in their own identities, some to keep from being alone, and some for my talent. Even my own father had used my musical talent to bolster his own sagging image, and when I lost weight he used me to show the world what a beautiful specimen he had fathered. He had taken credit for my victory in the child custody case even though it was I who was standing in front of the judge. Those three causes for pride: musical talent, beauty, and an intelligent wit had all been based on performance. Unless I performed, he was ashamed of me.

All of the men in my life had used me, but there had always been a payoff for me. I, like my mother before me, had chosen weak, ineffective males so I could remake them into "real men." As long as I was concentrating on *their* weak areas I didn't have to face my own. The bonus in this bizarre ritual was control. Having no control over my own life, I was to exercise control over their weak lives. My help was just the sunny side of control!

I had, after a year of discussion, agreed with my therapist that I needed to cut off all contact with my mother for at least one year. I saw how enmeshed I was with her and I knew that entanglement kept me from gaining a clear perspective on both the past and the present. I also knew that it was in my mother's interest to keep me from finding out which needs were mine and which needs were hers. I was sending large sums of money to her after receiving calls and letters telling me how she was one step from financial ruin. If the letters were six pages long, five of those pages would be itemizations of past due bills. I was sending the money out of guilt, but resenting every dollar. Unable to set boundaries with her, I finally wrote her a letter telling her I would neither be reading nor answering her letters. I would be neither calling her nor accepting calls from her for an unspecified amount of time: possibly more than a year.

Mama responded to my letter by writing her sister in Chicago with her tales of abandonment. Her sister had been receiving the same kind of letters I had been receiving, so when she heard I was "abandoning my own mother," she wrote to both Janine and me suggesting we have Mama committed. It was, she said, obvious Mama could not take care of herself.

What my aunt did not know was that Mama had a

friend several years her junior who was an alcoholic. Mama felt it was not his fault he couldn't work since he was "sick." She was taking the money we sent her and spending it on activities she shared with her friend. Mama was sure he was being called by God to preach, and she was going to help him quit drinking so he could answer God's calling.

I sent my aunt's letter to Mama, and that stopped the begging for money. But Mama tried communicating with me through my children, telling them how I had caused her to be hospitalized, near death, with a heart attack. She wrote letters to me that I returned unopened. She called and I hung up. She fought my decision as hard as she could and would not leave me alone. Sticking to my decision was the hardest test of my life, but I was successful.

Now, sitting in the airport waiting room, surrounded by dozens of happy families, I was anxious. It had been fourteen months since my break with my mother and I wondered if I was strong enough to see her again. The growth I had achieved was costly and I was protective of it. With nothing to occupy me but my thoughts, I sat and studied the faces of the other travelers: a habit that had won me innumerable slaps from my mother when I was a child.

I felt better about my appearance than I had in the last five years. I was thirty pounds lighter and had developed a new habit of walking several miles each day. My hair was frosted and longer, and I had begun to wear makeup again. My clothes were stylish and I didn't feel like I stuck out like a sore thumb.

Emotionally, I felt like I had crawled out of a long dark tunnel. Separated from my mother's influence, I felt capable of making my own decisions. I was becoming an emotional adult. During my separation from Mama, Janine had done an about-face, jumping in to fill the gap with compassion, understanding, and money for Mama. She had even written me letters berating me for my "un-Christ-like" behavior toward our mother. I understood the motivation behind Janine's change of attitude: by stepping out of the role as Mama's caretaker, I had upset the equilibrium in the family. As long as I was stepping in to meet Mama's needs and quiet her, Janine's life was peaceful and free of any responsibility as a daughter. My emotional enmeshment with Mama had also been serving Janine's interests. I eventually decided to withdraw from Janine until I felt strong enough to re-enter our relationship with some healthier ground rules.

I had set aside everyone else's needs and had concentrated on my own unmet needs. I had decided that it was, indeed, The Truth that would set me free, and I cleared my calendar to travel on my TRUTH JOURNEY. I had developed a daily routine to ensure my success: Oswald Chambers and the Scriptures with my coffee; walking in the cool of the morning before breakfast; shower and makeup after breakfast and vitamins; and journalizing my insights into bound, hardback journals. As I recorded my new insights, years of bitterness had been peeled away like layers of a stinky onion.

Thus far I had filled up three volumes. Three of the entries were significant:

UNtrue messages I learned from my parents

1. "There aren't any problems in our family. *You're* the problem for noticing there's a problem. (We have no problem with abuse. As long as we don't *talk* about it, there's no problem. You're the problem for talking about the abuse.")

2. "What's real doesn't matter. How things look to other people is what's important. God expects us to protect the image of our ministry."

3. "Adults are more important than kids, especially when it comes to feelings. *Your* feelings are never as important as *our* feelings."

4. "If we are upset, you are the cause. Therefore, you must also be the solution. If we are having marital problems, you are the cause. If we are having problems in our ministry, it is because of you, Marilyn. If we can't control our emotions, you are the reason. If we feel shame, it is your responsibility to do us proud and remove the shame from this family."

5. "There are different rules for parents than there are for kids. It is acceptable for us to act inappropriately in order to make you behave appropriately. You are accountable to us, but we are accountable to no one. It shows weakness for a parent to admit mistakes or ask forgiveness."

6. "There is a God, but He has very little to do with our daily lives. Like Daddy, He is absent, passive, and is too busy pleasing other people to have time for *you*. God is not ever going to defend or protect you – you're not worth it – and He is impotent as a power. Like Mama, He is erratic in His moods, impossible to please, capricious in His rule making, and vengeful. Not only does He wait for you to disobey, He waits for innocent mistakes. God is not to be depended upon because He's inconsistent. God won't be able to love you unless you're perfect."

7. "Your only worth to us – and to God – is in your performance."

8. "We are not responsible for our own behavior and feelings. Mama beats you because she is sick and you are bad. Daddy is weak because he can't handle stress. We are accountable only for how things *look*. We must all please God by *looking* spiritual. We must pay tithes so God will be obligated to bless us, and we must not confess our weaknesses to any other human being. It could start gossip."

9. "No one is allowed to say it straight. All of us must learn to speak in codes. That way no one will be accused of not being nice. We must keep the peace at all costs if we're to look spiritual. If a feeling isn't nice, it's unspiritual.

Therefore, we must never admit we have needs. The only need we have, Marilyn, is for *you to behave*."

10. "There's no free lunch in this world. If we give anything to you, it will never be free. We will expect something in return. Undying loyalty, permission to invade your privacy, and unquestioning obedience are acceptable payments. Nothing from *us* is free, and nothing from *God* is free. Our love is qualified, and so is God's love. God, like us, always keeps score."

How these UNtruths have played out in my life

• I'm tired spiritually, physically, and emotionally. I've spent my life being aware of others' needs, but have no clue about what my own needs are. I'm tired of performing: of being there for everyone else when he or she needs me, and then feeling my help was unappreciated.

• I hear me talking to myself, and it's always negative! My body has suffered with stress-related diseases: cancer, problems with my colon, eating disorders, insomnia, seizures, and on-going depression. I vacillate between perfectionism and sloth, rigid dieting and gluttony. I berate myself every bit as much as Mama berated me, and my compulsive behaviors will kill me if I can't get a handle on them. I can't seem to give myself a break.

• Most of my life has been spent seeking out relationships that end up reinforcing my shameful perception of myself. I seem to have this radar that attracts me to people who will eventually victimize me! I start out "helping" the person, don't get the payoff I feel I deserve, feel victimized and martyred, and then beat myself up for being so "stupid." It's a roller coaster ride that I seem compelled to repeat, even though it turns out the same most of the time. Could it be that with each repetition something deep inside me hopes I'll get it right this time [repetition compulsion]? Am I creating circumstances in order to rewrite the past?

• I search the Scriptures to know God in a more intimate way, but I don't really know the love of God. I accept it as truth because His Word says so, but it hasn't become concrete: it hasn't reached my emotions. I find it very easy to believe that God will heal a friend, but when I had breast cancer I didn't ask anyone to pray for a healing. I knew I was to blame for my own illness: I didn't eat right, I didn't exercise enough, I had unhealthy habits, etc. Why ask God to heal me if I wasn't perfect?

• I have, to my dismay, perpetuated the egregious lie that adults are allowed to live by a different set of rules than are their children. I have behaved badly in order to make my own children behave appropriately. I have communicated to them that their feelings as children are not as important as my adult feelings. I have called them names, taught them they couldn't measure up, and blamed them for my own lack of impulse control. I have taught them their worth was determined by their performance, and I've taught them to never be satisfied with their accomplishments. They have watched me blame everyone else for my own character flaws, and they have learned not to be accountable for their own. The sins of the father – and mother – have, indeed, been passed on to another generation. Now my fervent prayer is that God will not allow them to be passed on to yet another generation, even if it means I will never have grandchildren. I am depending upon God's mercy in this request.

• I have had three husbands and numerous other disastrous relationships with men. I have entered each relationship in a state of neurotic neediness, expecting each male to "make me happy," by filling all of my unmet needs from childhood. I have set myself up for certain failure. I've left each relationship because of my unmet needs, always thinking the next male would be the one. How misguided I've been! Only God can meet those needs. Only God can reach down with healing hands and heal the hurts of the past. Only God can give me worth and value. God is the only one who has the right – and the power – to validate me. And only God knows who He created me to be.

And then there was the hardest question of all:

IF GOD LOVED ME,

WHY DID HE ALLOW ME TO BE ABUSED?

If God was truly powerful, He could have stepped in at any given moment and stopped the abuse. He could, as many others have reasoned, step in and alleviate the suffering of millions who suffer. Is He really that uncaring? If so, it doesn't square with scripture.

Watching Fiddler on the Roof last week, I heard To-pol, in his role as Tevye talking to God about how busy He was with all those floods, earthquakes, and other natural disasters: those "little things You use to bring Your people back to You." I wondered if that's the only resource at God's disposal for keeping His children's attention. Or is it because "The heart of man is deceitfully wicked above all else" that pain is the only way God can reach it?

One thing I know for sure: it was no accident that I was born to my parents. I was fearfully and wonderfully made! God knew me, like He knew King David, before I was ever born. He created my inmost being; He knit me together in my mother's womb. My frame was not hidden from Him when I was made in the secret place. When I was woven together in the depths of the earth, His eyes saw my unformed body. All of the days ordained for me were written in His book before one of them came to be! In the darkness of my mother's womb, He knew what was ahead for me, and even then, He had made provision for me.

Scripture tells me that with every test God makes a way of escape, and throughout my life He has, indeed, been faithful to that promise. He gave me a kind Grandmother who, in her child-like faith, believed God would send

137

protective angels to me, and she never stopped praying for me. Who knows what I was spared because of those angels?

When I was only ten years old, He provided a Mexican surrogate mother, Madeline Diaz, who lived four houses away. Her house was my "safe place" and I ran to her for protection during Mama's more serious episodes. Madeline fed me homemade sopapillas with honey, and bedded me down on her couch until the storm was over.

He gave me a best friend, Patty, who was available whenever I needed her. Sometimes she hid me in her basement when my mother, in her rage, was looking for me. Patty was my soul mate during my most troubled years and we shared the pain as well as lots of good times.

God provided Miss Warden, my seventh grade teacher, who demonstrated *discipline without abuse*.

Then He provided my second surrogate mother, Margaret Trouissant, who took great delight in me and made me aware of my talents. Margaret redefined me in a positive way: she called it imagination instead of lying. And she has never stopped loving me or believing in me all these years.

In 1976, when I was about to make a terrible mistake, I received a letter from Margaret. In the right hand corner were printed these words: "Jesus Christ, the same yesterday, today, and forever." I remember being surprised that Margaret was a Christian all those years and I never knew it. As a result of her advice – handwritten in the familiar style of hers – I did not make the terrible mistake. But Margaret insists, to this day, that she never sent that letter. She says she never owned any stationery like that, and she's never read the material on the occult she sent me to the library to research. I know the letter was not a figment of my imagination because Alex read it, too. Her letter saved me from certain destruction, and I'm still wondering if it was written by one of those angels for which Grandma prayed.

Along the way God provided numerous people to

speak for Him, not the least of whom was Dr. Pugno. I still wonder if he was an angel. He left the county quickly after our encounter, and no one has ever been able to tell me where he went. What doctor leaves his residency without telling anyone where he'll be setting up his practice?

Then God provided another surrogate mother in Liliane Wright. She was already in place and was prepared to disciple me from the first week after I reached the end of myself. She was familiar with long-term consequences of child abuse, and she taught me lovingly, but firmly, always holding me accountable for what I already knew but was not yet putting into practice. She and Lew were sent to help Alex and me when there seemed to be no hope for us. She still is the one I call when I need a mother.

And God provided Anne when I needed a sister in the Lord. She always took me back to *What does Scripture say about that?* She's a faithful prayer partner who follows up her prayers with phone calls to find out what miracle God did for me each day. Together we have experienced great pain and great blessings. She and other gifts of friendship from God have been my prayer support through years of ups and downs, and all of them love me for who I am.

Yes, God allowed great pain in my life; but He balanced the pain with merciful surrogates who filled the comfort gaps left by my own family members. He never promised an easy life, but He did promise He would never leave me, and He hasn't. At times when I needed the human factor, He has provided loving, supportive people to put their arms around me and listen to my feelings without judging me. He has provided human beings that were capable of unqualified love: something I never would have understood about *God's* love if I had never experienced it with *human* love.

The Scriptures are full of hurting people: some of them were rescued *out of* the den, and some, like Daniel, were rescued *in* the den. The theology I heard, as a child, was wrong: your life does *not* become problem-free when you come to Christ. God never promised a pain-free life. In fact, He promised we would know pain just as Jesus knew pain. Some of my pain was the natural consequence of disobedience on my parents' part. Some of it was self-inflicted. Some of it was the consequences of living in a fallen world. And some of it I'll probably never understand, but that's ok now. No longer do I need all of my questions answered. I have been freed from that bondage.

God's ways are definitely beyond human understanding. Wiser people than I have yet to define God. If I had all the answers, I wouldn't need to walk by faith. I pray for <u>wisdom</u> to know what can be changed, <u>courage</u> to change what I'm able to change and <u>serenity</u> to accept what is in God's hands. As I accept responsibility for my own behavior, trust God for healing, and live one day at a time, I find I have less and less need to know all the whys and wherefores.

I am responsible only for accepting where God put me at birth, the body and mind He gave me, and for being a good steward of the talents and gifts He gave me. I am <u>not</u> responsible for God's decisions. I am <u>not</u> responsible for explaining God's ways. I am only responsible for the part of God that He reveals to me, and the only answers I need are the ones He chooses, in His grace, to give.

I know He has a plan for my life. Jeremiah 29:11 tells me so. His plans are not to harm me, but to give me hope and a future. The timing of my life was unique, and was ordained by God. I was neither an accident to my parents, nor an inconvenience to my Heavenly Father. And God did not create a freak when He created me. I was in the right place at the right time: my timing was unique and deliberate. Only when I see Him face-to-face will I have all the answers.

~~~

Two years of doing my homework had left me feeling I had a good understanding of not only the unhealthy family dynamics that had tainted my perception of myself, but also some healthy tools to use as I tried to build new, healthier relationships. Isolated from Mama's influence, I had begun to find out who I was apart from her. I had learned *how* to think, not *what* to think. And I was at peace with God and comfortable with myself. Life wasn't perfect, but it was workable.

Now it was time to see how much I had really learned about setting boundaries – not walls to keep Mother out, but property lines to define where she ends and I begin. It was time to re-establish contact with my mother. No longer did I feel the need to have a "Mama." In fact, I didn't really need anything at all from her, not even an admission of her abuse. I was now able to understand that Mother would never change, and if she couldn't remember the abuse, it was her way of protecting herself. I knew it had occurred. I had forgiven her – I had relinquished my "right" to punish her – the way God had forgiven me. No longer was I her needy child desperately seeking her approval: I approved of myself. And no longer did I see her as a monster that was to be blamed for all my ills. That's how I knew the time was right.

I picked up my suitcase and headed for the boarding ramp. I hadn't seen my mother in five years. I hadn't had any communication with her for fourteen months. I felt the tightness in my stomach I always experienced when I talked to Mother. I whispered a prayer for God to go before me and prepare the way.

It was lunchtime when the jet started circling over El Paso International Airport. I looked out the window at the brown, dry desert and remembered all the childhood days I had spent sweating in the hot sun. The pilot's voice told us it was sunny and 110 degrees in El Paso. I was glad I didn't have to leave the air-conditioned airport during my two-hour lunch with her.

As we disembarked from the plane, I looked for Mother's face, and when I didn't see her I felt relieved. Maybe she had changed her mind. Strange, though: she had sounded so eager to see me when I had called her on my way to Austin five days ago. Maybe she's just late, I thought. She's always late for everything. That's one of the reasons she and Daddy used to fight so much. I decided to walk down the long hallway and find a coffee shop. It had been six hours since breakfast and I was hungry.

As I made my way through the crowds I glanced at each shop window thinking maybe I should pick up a souvenir for Alex. I noticed an old woman, all bent over, looking frantically inside each shop door. I knew how it felt to be lost, and I felt immediate compassion for this poor confused woman. She was traveling in my direction, but was still too far away for conversation. I decided I would offer to help her find whatever she was searching for when she got closer. But before I could open my mouth to offer help, our eyes met and her face broke out into the biggest smile I had ever seen. I thought she had recognized some one behind me, so I kept walking.

"Marilyn!" she screamed. "Honey, I thought I'd never find you!" She was still fifty feet away and I looked hard to see her face. The poor old woman was my mother! As we reached each other she grabbed me and hugged me like her life depended on it. Still in shock at the aging that had changed her, I hugged her back and lied as she asked me how she looked. "You look good," I said. "You look as young and beautiful as ever." It was an act of kindness to the woman who had always feared looking her age.

Mother clung to me like she was afraid I'd change my mind and leave before we had lunch. We had trouble fitting through the restaurant door because she wouldn't let go of my arm. The hostess was someone she knew and she beamed as she informed the girl that her "daughter from California" had come all the way to El Paso to visit her. The girl said that was wonderful, and then asked how long I would be staying. I said two hours. After we were seated at our table, Mother asked me why I had to say "two hours." She said people were always commenting on how neither of her daughters ever visits, and they wondered why.

"Do you tell them it's because you won't allow anyone inside your trailer, Mother?" I asked calmly, but resolutely. Several years before, my cousins from Chicago, Texas, and California had visited Mother and then had reported to Aunt Olivia in Chicago the thousands of newspapers piled up. Mother had only a pathway from the front door to the rear of the trailer and all of her furniture except the piano was hidden under piles of papers. It had been after that visit that Aunt Olivia asked Janine and me to have Mother committed. It had also been the last time Mother allowed anyone to enter her trailer. Mark, her own grandson, had driven to Texas to visit with her, but she had made him stay in a motel.

"Don't bring that up," she answered as she reached into her purse for the sandwich she had brought to the restaurant. "We don't have much time, Mar – I mean April. It's so hard to remember to call you April. Tell me again why you changed your name, honey," she said with a mouthful of Spam sandwich.

"Mother, my legal name has been M. April for fifteen years. I had it legally changed because no one in California has ever known me by any other name. I wrote poetry and songs using that name from the time I was eleven, even before I became an entertainer using the name of 'April.' Also, when I founded C.O.P.E. I was known to everyone as April."

"But why didn't you keep the name I gave you?" she asked pathetically.

"Don't you remember, Mother? You asked me not to get rid of 'Marilyn,' and I didn't. The only name I changed was my middle name: 'Joyce.'"

"Oh, so your first name is still Marilyn?"

"Yes, Mother, but I don't use it. I just use the initial, like you do. Your first name is Claire, but you've always used C. Elise, right?"

"Oh, well, that's not so bad," she said with relief in her voice. It was as if she was searching for assurance that I had not completely disowned her, and the name issue was symbolic of that assurance.

"Mother, I never asked you to call me anything but what you named me." It hurt me to see her trying so hard. It was obvious to me that the fourteen-month separation had left her afraid of offending me. In that moment, The Holy Spirit opened my eyes and let me see – just for a second – how old and utterly alone she was. True, her lifestyle had caused her to keep people out of her home, but I saw a pitiful woman sitting before me whose entire life had been spent in bondage to fear. Even as a child she had lived in fear that someone would find out about her alcoholic father: his shameful behavior, his rages, his loss of identity as he lost everything he owned in the Depression. And then when she lost her security – her over-indulgent, over-protective mother – she feared living life without her. It was only a brief moment, but in that camera-shot moment I saw sixty-seven years of behavior motivated by fear. I felt genuine compassion for Mother.

"Marilyn," she said as she reached across the table to touch my arm – that was her way of making sure I was paying attention to her – "about those beatings you accused me of."

I had already decided I would not bring up the subject; but, if she brought it up, I was prepared to stand calmly and firmly in the truth. I had decided not to encourage her denial by being dishonest and saying it didn't matter. It did matter! Now I waited to hear her, once again, tell me how I had imagined all those beatings.

"I swear to you, honey, I honestly didn't remember ever hitting you. But I called Janine, and she told me about several incidents she remembered. I know, now, you were not making it all up."

Not only were her words a total shock to me, so was the way she was looking me straight in the eyes as she talked. In fact, all through our conversation she had actually been paying attention to me! Her mind was clear, her usual compulsion to repeatedly interrupt was gone, and she was one hundred percent present! She had never been like that before, and I knew it was a gift from God: a miracle *just for me*.

"No, Mother," I said in a kind, but firm voice, "I was not making it up. It did happen. You know, Mother, I can understand why you had so much difficulty coping with parenthood; but what I can't understand is why you never tried to get help for yourself. I hold you responsible for what you did to me, and, also, for not getting help for yourself. That was your responsibility."

"I can't believe I treated you so badly, Honey. The only thing I can think of to explain it is how sick I was with those migraine headaches. And you were so hard to handle. I just didn't know how to handle you."

"There were books available, Mother. Books that would have taught you how to parent: books that, if you had gone to the library and checked them out, would have identified me as a child with ADHD. There was help available to you, if you had looked for help. It was your responsibility to look for help. *You* were the parent. *You* were the one who couldn't cope. The Bible says I was a gift to you from God, Mother: a heritage of the Lord! God holds you responsible for the heritage He gave you!"

"But your father didn't help me at all, Marilyn. He left the house and left me to handle all the problems. He should have helped me!" she pleaded.

"Mother, you are not responsible for Daddy's behavior. You are only responsible for your own. You were the mother. It was your responsibility to learn all you could about your own problems that kept you from being a mother to me. You were responsible for putting my needs before your own. You raised me to feel responsible for *your* needs! Instead of you taking care of my needs, I was expected to take care of your needs. That's backwards! Daddy's abdication of his responsibilities didn't absolve you of your God-given responsibilities to your babies! We will all stand alone before Jesus, not as half of a team. We will be judged alone, Mother." My voice was still gentle, but firm.

"Oh, if only – "

"No, Mother. Not if only! That's how you have always escaped honest confrontation. There is no 'if only.' There is only what was and what is. That's reality. You can't change the past. You can only acknowledge past mistakes and change the present."

"You know that I've always loved you, don't you, Marilyn?" she asked like a hurt child implores.

"No, Mother. I have never *felt* your love."

"Oh Marilyn! Don't say that!" she cried. "I'm telling you I love you!"

"Mother, you taught me a saying: 'Talk is cheap.' It will take more far more than words to fix what's wrong between us. If you really love me, and you want me to believe it, then you will show me."

"How can I show you?" she asked with genuine sincerity.

"By respecting my boundaries, Mother."

"What does that mean?"

"It means that I am a separate person from you. If I disagree with you, it just means I, another human being, have a different view than you do. It *doesn't* mean something is wrong with me. It doesn't mean something is wrong with you, either. It just means we have a different opinion. My opinions are not a reflection of your worth, Mother. They're just my opinions."

"You were always so smart, Marilyn. Always one step ahead of me. It made me feel dumb. I'm not sure I understand what you want from me."

"Mother, everyone has a language of love. For example: a woman cooks her husband's favorite meal because she wants to express how much she loves him. But he doesn't understand what she's trying to communicate. He just thinks she likes to cook. He has a *different* language than she does. What would really communicate love to him would be a new negligee and a surprise afternoon love-making session. Does that help you understand?" She nodded it did.

"The ways you could communicate respect and love for me would be by *not* interrupting me when I'm trying to talk to you; not telling me all the details of your relationship with the latest preacher protégé. When I tell you I don't want to hear the details, you could respect my wishes and talk about something else. Simple courtesy would go a long way, too: asking me how I am, how my children are instead of jumping in to tell me all your problems. Do you realize you *never ask about me*, Mother? Not even when I'm paying for the call? Didn't you ever wonder *why* I was calling you?"

"I guess I've been pretty selfish, haven't I? Will you forgive me for hurting you, Marilyn?" she asked cautiously. "Can you forgive me?"

"Mother, I forgave you two years ago. But it's nice to hear you ask."

"I notice you don't call me Mama anymore. What happened to Mama?"

"I've grown up, Mother. I'm not a child anymore."

"Does that mean you don't love me anymore?" The look on her face almost made me cry. It was as if her whole life hung on my answer.

"Mother, I love you because you're my mother. I honor you because God tells me to honor my mother. But most of my life I've been afraid of you – not just afraid of getting hit. I was afraid you would *always* be controlling my thoughts and feelings. When I left home I only knew *what* to think. You never allowed me to make any of my own decisions, so I never learned *how* to think. I was afraid I would never measure up to your expectations, and I didn't. And I was afraid I'd end up treating my own children the way you treated me. I did, for a long time, but then I got help. I got help for myself, and I got help for them. Now that I'm not afraid of you anymore, I am free to love you."

"You and Janine were so different. I never had to worry about her. She seemed to do everything right, and you rebelled."

"Mother, why do you think Janine has had three failed marriages? Why do you think she's constantly striving for more college degrees, more money and the status it brings? Why do you think she's killing herself with compulsive exercise? She hasn't had a period for ten years because of all the aerobics classes she teaches each day. She talks about cosmetic surgery: tummy tucks, face lifts, eye lifts and she's been anorexic for years! Didn't you ever wonder why she was always such a perfectionist, so compelled to excel in everything she did?"

"No, but I did wonder why she was so mean. Remember when she said we had to have an appointment to come to her house? She lived in the same city!"

"She was trying to break away from her parents, Mother. She was fighting for her identity. She was trying to set boundaries: to find out where you and Daddy ended and where she began as a person. Daddy held her so close that she had to get angry in order to break away. It was the only way she could survive. Janine came into adulthood with just as many problems as I did; she just handled them differently."

"I've really made a mess of things, haven't I? I'm so sorry I wasn't a better mother, Marilyn. If I could go back and do it over, I'd do a better job."

"You can't go back, Mother. None of us can. But we can move forward. We can use whatever time we have left to make the present happier. I'm willing to try if you are, but I'm **not** willing to go back to the way we **were**. I have limitations now, and you'll have to respect them if you want a relationship."

Mother nodded through her tears that she was willing to try to build a relationship with new guidelines. She waited at the window of the airport until I disappeared in the sky.

On the trip home I felt like a heavy burden had been lifted off my shoulders. I knew God had blessed me with something few abused children ever get: an admission of guilt, a request of forgiveness, and a chance to honestly confront the abusing parent with how her abuse had affected my life. I replayed the entire two hours I had spent with

Mother, and it became crystal clear that I had possessed two kinds of peace the entire time. I had the peace that had come as a result of reaching out for help, confronting my problems, and doing painful homework on my own self. It was a peace that had come from having the courage to confront myself. It was a confident satisfaction: a job well done. It was an *earned* peace.

Then there was the peace that passes human understanding: God's peace. I can never earn it, but I can obstruct it through disobedience.

God had wrapped His arms around me, called me by name, and sat on the seat next to mine. He had never left me for one moment. He had gone before me, prepared Mother with an open heart and a lucid mind. He had ordered every step of my journey, doing far more than I ever dreamed or hoped. He had given me closure for my wounds, confidence for my journey, and hope for the future.

He was, after all, my "Heavenly Daddy," and I finally felt like "Daddy's girl." As talked about in Zephaniah 3:17, I felt Him *taking great delight in me, quieting me with His love, and rejoicing over me with singing*.

It was exactly 10:00 p.m. on that Sunday night in March. The theme for Charles Stanley's "In Touch" had just begun and I was reaching for the phone to shut off the ringer for the night.

"Is this Marilyn? Is this Elise's daughter?" the man's voice asked hesitantly.

"Yes, this is Marilyn." My gut told me something was wrong, but I kept my composure.

"This is Pastor Morales, your mother's pastor. I'm calling with some bad news, Marilyn."

I felt my legs weaken. I wanted to run away.

I sat down as Mama's pastor explained how she had stayed after evening service to practice special music for the next Sunday. As she was exiting the church and crossing the street a car running with no lights had come out of no where and hit her at 65 miles per hour. She was still in intensive care and wasn't expected to live through the night.

"Pastor, please don't leave my mother. Even if she's not conscious, please don't let her be alone," I begged.

"Oh no, Mija. I won't leave Mama." He broke into tears and lost his pastoral composure as he spoke. "I'm sorry. This is so sad, Marilyn. Your mom, she means so much to all of us. I don't understand how God could let this happen, but I think I should get off the phone now. I know the doctor that's in charge of her will be trying to call you."

"Thank you for calling, Pastor."

I don't remember hanging up the phone. The room was spinning and everything within me wanted to run away.

But I do remember the phone ringing again and again, each time the doctor telling me about the horrible injuries Mama had sustained, the three operations, and how all we could do now was wait.

I sat in my chair staring at the wall in front of me. No logical thoughts ran through my mind. All I could hear was a tiny girl screaming, "I don't want to be an orphan!" over and over. Then I heard a grown woman crying the same words as she convulsed in tears. It sounded like me, but felt removed, as if I was listening to another person. I felt detached from reality – like I was floating in troubled waters.

I called Janine to let her know Mama was critical, and in her shocked condition, she said, "Marilyn, if she dies, leave a message on my machine. I've got to get some sleep."

At 3:00 a.m. the phone rang again, and before my husband could answer it I was already wailing, "No, God! No, God!"

Mama was dead.

I was an orphan.

I called Janine and left a message on her machine that our mother was dead. Then I called the airlines to book a ticket to El Paso, knowing I would have no help from Janine handling Mama's affairs or going through years of newspapers.

At 7:00 a.m. I was in the happiest place I've ever been. Then I heard my husband's voice forcing me out of my dream, telling me it was time to get up and drive to the airport. From the deepest part of me a wail started and mushroomed to a deafening pitch. I felt his arms around me, rocking me as I lost control of all those inhibitions that had served me so well throughout my life. No defenses left now – just primal screams that had been stored so deep and so long.

"I was in such a happy place, and you woke me up and now I know that my Mama is dead!" I accused. I felt totally alone and abandoned by everyone including God. How could He allow her to be killed in such a violent manner?

It took every ounce of strength I had to keep my mind from visualizing Mama being torn apart by a two-thousand-pound murder machine. I searched for my index card that had Philippians 4:8-9 written on it, and I looked at it over and over. I tried to make sense of it, but my mind was on its own. I kept thinking, "That's why Mama wasn't home when I called tonight."

Before I could leave for El Paso, people I didn't know were calling me to tell how my mother had brought them to the Lord – how, in her slippers, she had gone door to door asking people to come to church with her. They told of new lives now, devoid of drugs, prostitution, and gangs since accepting Jesus as their Lord and Savior, and all attributed their salvation to the persistence of Mama. It seemed the phone would ring the moment one call would end, all callers testifying to my mother's obedience to The Great Commission.

When my son John and I arrived at Mama's trailer there were people waiting to tell me how my mother had cared for their souls when no one else cared. It was an awesome experience to "see" Mama through the eyes of others. She had been a mother to many others even though she had not been able to be a mother to me.

On the day of Mama's funeral I was exhausted beyond explanation. John and I had spent five days cleaning out 25 years of newspapers and organizing her belongings for a yard sale. I'll never know how I managed to take care of all the necessary details in the middle of such chaos, but I did. Janine and her daughter showed up three hours before the funeral, and taking one look at the bad shape I was in, she took charge.

"Marilyn, I've rented a motel room and I'm taking you there. You want to look your best at the funeral and you won't be able to do any grooming in this place. Let's go!"

It was a thoughtful gesture and it gave us time to be alone before we buried our mother. Janine couldn't get past the "visual" of Mama being mangled, and she couldn't understand why God would allow such a horrible thing to happen to one of His children. By this time, I had gained a new perspective. I remembered how fearful Mama had been of dying a long, painful cancer death, so I saw her quick death as a blessing from God.

When we arrived at the mission there were so many people attending Mama's funeral that it had to be moved to the big church. People had come from several states, as far away as Illinois. There were familiar members from the churches Daddy had pastored, and unfamiliar faces beaming with recognition as I walked inside. I was astonished when I saw all the huge floral arrangements at the front of the church. It looked like a president had died. And people kept stopping me to tell me how Mama had so persistently witnessed to them that they had finally given in and come to church with her. I lost count of Mama's spiritual children – there were so many whose lives Mama had touched.

Even the newspaper ran a front-page story telling about this woman who "did more than most pastors do" to help the down-and-outs of El Paso.

All of those people through the years that Mama had talked about – faceless names I thought I'd never meet – I met all of them that day. And I recognized all of their names because Mama had told me about each of them receiving Christ. She had always been most animated when telling me about a "new soul for The Kingdom."

After we sang two of Mama's favorite hymns and had listened to "I Bowed on My Knees and Cried 'Holy'," I rose and walked to the podium. It was time to talk about

Mama and her life. I looked out on a sea of redeemed humanity and realized Mama's life was not about her inability to control her anger, or her obsession with newspapers. Jesus wouldn't care one bit that she wasn't a good housekeeper or cook. He wouldn't even care that she was so age-conscious. Her life would not be measured by her failures, but by her obedience to her Lord.

Radiant brown Mexican faces stared back at me. Faces that once were covered in shame, chained by drugs and prostitution, full of fear from gang retribution – now they beamed with the love of Jesus and love for my mother. They were all ages – parents with children and grandchildren – all eager to testify on Mama's behalf.

Many times I had read about God putting us "on eagles' wings" where we would run and not be weary, walk and not faint. But I gained a new understanding of that reality as I opened my mouth to speak. What Robert Browning called "solemn joy" and the Bible calls "joy unspeakable" came over me and rejuvenated every part of my being.

I felt privileged to stand in front of my mother's *other children* and speak on her behalf.

"I stand before you today to say I'm proud to be the daughter of Elise Morston. I'm proud to look at all her jewels in this audience. Someday she will lay each of you at the feet of Jesus as a precious jewel." Faces beamed as each one recognized I was speaking about him or her.

"To those of you who have not yet met Jesus – who have not yet been reborn into a new creation, I ask you: Some day you will be gone and your children may have to speak on your behalf. What will they be able to say about your life? Will they be able, as I am, to say your life counted for God? Will they be able to say without reserve that you are in the Presence of God? I pray they will. Thank you for coming to honor my mother."

That night I reflected on the history of two unlikely friends: Mama and myself. I wept with gratitude that God had allowed her to live long enough for us to become friends. She wasn't a mother to me, but she had been a mother to countless others at a time when they needed help. She gave what she had to give, and what she didn't have she couldn't give to me.

I was grateful I had no regrets at all. So many others I had known were filled with remorse over words spoken or not spoken, deeds done or not done. I had no regrets! I felt total peace about my part in our relationship, and had an understanding about her part in it. I had listened to her when no one else would; I had sacrificed monetarily to make sure she had her needs filled; and I had reached a place inside myself where I found genuine affection for the woman who gave me life. God had ordered my steps and made sure I would not be left with unfinished business when she died. For that gift I would always praise Him.

I saw the wisdom of our fourteen-month separation, for without it I would never have found myself. We would not have been able to redefine our relationship before she died. I saw my mother as God saw her: a damaged soul with darkened perception. She honestly thought every thing she had done – even keeping up appearances – had been for the glory of God. She had, in effect, "protected God's image" by keeping so many secrets. And what was too painful to remember, she had simply forgotten.

I picked up her calendars and started reading the details of her life. Because her memory failed, she was in the habit of writing down all the events of her life, including every time I had called her, on her wall calendar. I looked at February's calendar and saw a minuscule note in her cramped handwriting. It said, *"Marilyn: Psalms 32:8"* Chills raced through my body as I reached for my Bible.

"I will instruct you and teach you in the way you should go; I will guide you with My eye."

Under the scripture reference on her calendar was an 800 number and the words *"Good for two months only."* I called the 800 number and discovered Mama had accepted one of those "we'll-pay-the-first-two-months-for-you" accidental death policies for an enormous amount of coverage. Mama, who had spent all of her life scratching for the next dime, had unknowingly left Janine and I a small fortune. She never paid a dime for the policy because she was killed within those two free months.

In addition, I discovered three insurance policies she had paid on for years – policies that named me as beneficiary. Tucked inside one of them was the only poem my mother ever wrote: a poem about her love for me! I wept as I tried to read her handwriting – all those words she could never say to me were written for me to find. She had known, all along, the pain I had suffered as a result of childhood! She had known how hard I had worked at our relationship, and what sacrifices I had made to ensure her material needs were met. She had planned all those years to say "Thank You" in a way that *showed* me her gratitude. She did, after all, teach me that "Talk is cheap." And here was Mama's offering in what she saw as my "language of love:" Poetry.

Oddly enough, I never thought how much money I had. I thought only of how my God had honored Mama's faithfulness by giving her something to leave behind for both of her children. I thought of David asking if there was anyone of the house of Jonathan whom he might honor. I thought of how much I'd enjoy Mother's Day as I gave large sums of money to the Gideons in Mama's name. It gave me great pleasure to know that even though Mama was not here, she would still be reaching people for Jesus through the money she left behind.

And she left me this old steamer trunk. I'm sure she did not remember half of what was in here – valuable treasures one could only dream of receiving: Antique dolls that had belonged to her own mother, crystal salvaged from

157

the fire, and other family heirlooms, all ordered to be burned after my grandmother died. There were letters written between my mother and her sister, art drawings my mother left behind, and loads of records that would help me as I did the family genealogy. My own mother and her father had hidden this trunk from my grandmother's sisters, and then Mama had dragged it through more than fifty years of traveling.

I looked at all the generations of photos she left behind – some of the photos were on metal – and I actually felt grateful she was such a pack rat. I looked through her art book and marveled at her talent. Neither of her daughters had ever seen any of her drawings. I looked through Mama's high school yearbooks and lived her teenage years through the pictures and writings. I held her awards for Latin Champion of Lee County and I marveled at her intelligence.

I read all of the baby cards people sent her when I was born, all the birthday cards through the years from Grandma Morston, Aunt Olivia and other relatives. I experienced my own childhood going through all the memoirs she had packed away in her father's ship trunk. I read old documents and hundreds of letters that gave me a complete understanding of the pain Mama had experienced in her own childhood, and I marveled that she had survived as well as she had.

And then I called Mary, Mama's closest friend for sixty-five years.

"Oh, Marilyn! You have your mother's laugh! It brings back such wonderful memories of our times together!" she exclaimed. "You know your mother was so much fun to be around. She even laughed at her own jokes, just like you do!"

Yes, Mary knew the "real" Elise and now I did, too. She was a sensitive child raised by fearful parents who were unable to express any emotion except anger and shame. She was curious, intelligent, talented, and child-like with her emotions. She was always afraid she wouldn't measure up to anyone's expectations, including God's, so she kept up appearances. She was ebullient, well-liked, and as she got older, she cared deeply about damaged souls. She made some serious mistakes along the way, but was committed to Jesus. In the end, as she stood before Him, I know that is all that really mattered.

Goodbye, Mama. I'm glad you're finally whole!

Goodbye, Daddy. Hope there's a fishin' hole in Heaven!

Hello, Marilyn. Hello, April. Yes, Jesus loves you, and I am finally at peace with both of you.